WINNING

WITH

FUTURES

WINNING
WITH
FUTURES

The Smart Way to Recognize

Opportunities, Calculate Risk,

and Maximize Profits

MICHAEL C. THOMSETT

American Management Association

New York • Atlanta • Brussels • Chicago • Mexico City • San Francisco
Shanghai • Tokyo • Toronto • Washington, D.C.

Special discounts on bulk quantities of AMACOM books are available to corporations, professional associations, and other organizations. For details, contact Special Sales Department, AMACOM, a division of American Management Association, 1601 Broadway, New York, NY 10019.
Tel.: 212–903–8316. Fax: 212–903–8083.
Web site: www.amacombooks.org

Library of Congress Cataloging-in-Publication Data

Thomsett, Michael C.
   Winning with futures : the smart way to recognize opportunities, calculate risk, and maximize profits / Michael C. Thomsett.
       p.   cm.
   Includes index.
   ISBN-13: 978-0-8144-0987-9
   ISBN-10: 0-8144-0987-3
   1. Futures.   2. Futures market.   3. Investments.   I. Title.

   HG6024.A3T478   2009
   332.64'52—dc22

                                        2008026399

Printing number

10   9   8   7   6   5   4   3   2   1

CONTENTS

PREFACE

Virtually anyone can become adept in the futures market. With practice and study, what may seem a complex and high-risk market can be tailored to fit a niche for virtually any investor seeking profit opportunities and diversification. You have to realize, however, that risks vary, and any entry into this market should be a sensible and suitable match between the avenue you pick and your personal level of risk tolerance.

A *future* is a contract granting its buyer the right to buy a specified amount of a commodity, shares in a stock market index, or a foreign currency. Very few purchasers of futures actually take possession of the commodity underlying the contract. Most futures trading is undertaken with the goal of closing out the contract at a favorable price.

In comparison, an *option* is a contract on stocks and indices. Most stock-related options are traded speculatively. A long position is entered hoping its value will rise so that the option can be closed at a profit. Short sellers have the opposite goal, and will sell an option hoping the stock's value will fall. When that happens, the option can be bought and closed at a lower price. Options traders also use options to protect long stock positions or to swing trade in the very short term.

Both futures and options can be high risk or highly conservative, depending on how they are used. Futures are often perceived as very high risk. However, alternative methods of investing in the futures market can mitigate the risk, and futures can be effective portfolio hedging tools; trading and cyclical choices; and in many situations, used to take advantage of short-term cyclical changes.

The terms "futures" and "commodities" are used interchangeably in the market; however, an accurate definition makes a distinction between all futures contracts, which may be written on a range of commodities as well as financial instruments and market indices. A commodity in the strict sense excludes currencies and indices and is limited to energy, grains and oilseeds, livestock, lumber, precious metals, and imported materials.

This book is aimed at the novice, including experienced stock market investors with little or no knowledge about the futures market. The intention of this book is to explain the market in a spectrum of risks and opportunities, so that you will be able to make an informed decision about how to enter this market, and how your own acceptable risk levels match to futures speculation.

You can also employ these interesting instruments to diversify a stock portfolio, or to hedge against other positions. For example, if you own shares of an oil company stock, a futures contract anticipating a drop in oil prices works as a possible hedge. If the stock value falls, the value of the future may offset the loss. Many opportunities like this exist. Another example involves the use of futures on foreign currency. If the U.S. stock market is going to suffer from the effects of exchange rates, you can pick stocks defensively (or limit your investments to companies doing most of their business in other countries). You can also hedge your stock portfolio by taking positions in currency futures.

The point is that there are many ways to augment or protect stock positions in your portfolio, and futures contracts may play a part in that. Few investors today can safely put all their money into stocks and simply wait for long-term appreciation. This traditional model (often called *value investing*) will work in some companies, and is suitable for some people. But today, many investors are realizing that their portfolio can be further enhanced and diversified by expanding beyond stocks. This means using options, exchange-traded funds (ETFs) and traditional mutual funds, real estate, and of course, futures—all as part of a more sophisticated portfolio strategy. By reaching not only an expanded menu of products, but an international and multisector strategy, you can compete today in a way that, in the past, only large institutional investors could.

This expanded capability has been made both accessible and

affordable through the Internet. In the past, many markets like the futures exchanges were simply too expensive for those with modest capital resources; and the cost of transacting was so prohibitive that most people could not consider futures and similar products as viable instruments. Today, this has all changed. As long as you are able to educate yourself about the risks, strategies, and opportunities, all markets have become available.

The speed and low cost of modern investing, made possible by the Internet, represents an incredible revolution in the investing world. It only remains for the average investor to gain the knowledge needed to effectively enter into new markets. Only with a good working understanding of the market can you (a) identify risk and opportunity, (b) select appropriate strategies, given your risk profile, and (c) begin an expanded program of allocating resources in your portfolio beyond the traditional ownership of stock.

In *Winning with Futures*, you find a comprehensive but basic introduction to this market. The format and presentation are designed to help answer your questions and to find additional resources to expand your study of the futures market. The AMACOM series of "Winning with . . ." books are all designed in the same way. The objective in this series is to provide readers with a complete, nontechnical, and practical overview of a specific investment. The result is that you, as the reader, will gain the confidence and knowledge you need to ask the right questions. The first of these, of course, is How do I know that the market is appropriate for me? This appropriate and key question should always serve as your starting point. In this and other books in the series, this is the question that is constantly present in all discussions. These books are reader-oriented and based on the assumption that you can only answer this key question if you have all the information you need to understand the advantages, risks, and strategic requirements of investing.

Many investors have simply given up trying to diversify their portfolio because they cannot find basic information about markets beyond the basic stock-based strategies. This explains the popularity of mutual funds over the past half century. As successful and profitable as mutual funds have been, however, for many investors there are other alternatives worth exploring. This is why the "Winning with . . ." series was started; it fills an important niche in investment education by providing the essentials on many different markets. In *Winning with Futures,* you will not find technical jargon or complex formulas. You will find basic, nontechnical, and practical advice and information, enabling you to take the next step for yourself.

WINNING
WITH
FUTURES

PART 1

KNOWING YOUR MARKET

```
.2752   3.2088   -.0040   16,542   5 Yr. Treasury Not
.2642   3.2075   -.0037   26,569   June    111-087 111
                                    Sept    110-285 110
Jol. 5 Do1 00.
    G   3.0307   -.0330   19,962   2 Yr. Treasury Note
        3.0217   -.0250   98,525   June    106-007 106-0
                                    30 Day Federal Fund.
11.290   .217   15,673   April   97.735   97.7
11.329   .226   140,673  May     97,930   97.96
1.492    .212   81,584
1.569    .180   66,643   1 Month Libor (CME)-$3
504      .160   55,727   May     97.2100 97.230(
729      .160   43,819   June    97.2850 97.2950

                        Eurodollar (CME)-$1,000.0
                        May     97.1450 97.1925
                        June    97.1200 97.2150
22.75   104,533  Sept   97.0400 97.1500
22.75   567,041  Dec    96.8600 96.9700

03      191   Currency Futures
```

WHAT IS A FUTURES CONTRACT?

f you could know the future value of anything, you would naturally be able to get rich. In all public markets, investors and traders share this common dream, and the anticipation of future price movement dictates how and where investment decisions get made. In fact, the *futures* market is a formalized version of this forward-looking pattern. But it involves commodities, indices, and financial instruments rather than stocks.

One famous writer spoke of the future as "That period of time in which our affairs prosper, our friends are true and our happiness is assured."[1] This makes an important point about all forms of investing. Optimism is often a ruling force, and those investors who look optimistically to the future expect prices to rise, hopefully immediately after they take up a position in the stock, bond, or futures contract.

As a philosophy of investing, the futures market contains a never-ending series of price estimates for future goods: oil, grain, livestock, metals, coffee, currency exchange, and even stocks. Futures contracts set a price of future delivery. This does not mean that if you buy a futures contract, you expect to actually take delivery of the product involved; it does mean that if the actual price moves higher than the fixed price of the futures contract, you can sell that contract and take a profit.

This is only one basic explanation of how futures contracts work and are traded. The variations involve not only different positions (long or short) but different structures as well (direct trades, indices, or exchange-traded funds, for example).

Essential Definitions

A good starting point is to carefully define the *futures contract*. This is an agreement involving the purchase and sale of a specified amount of a commodity (or index, currency, or other asset of value). The contract sets the value as well as the delivery date; it is *standardized*, meaning that the expiration cycles are set ahead of time, monthly or quarterly. So delivery occurs every three months. The reason for standardizing futures contracts is to make them more easily exchanged in the market. When every futures contract is set by date and amount, traders have an efficient market and can easily find the value of every existing contract. The futures contract can only be bought or sold on the futures exchange, and only a member of that exchange can execute the transaction.

In a futures contract, a good-faith margin deposit is required at the time the contract is originated. The basic transaction is speculative, but it is based on anticipation of price movement. If you buy a futures contract and the value of the underlying commodity rises, then the value of that contract will rise as well. However, you can take out your profits or close out the contract whenever you want. This feature, *escapability*, makes futures speculation relatively easy, so that speculation in futures works very much like speculation in the options market.

Investors buy and sell futures contracts for several reasons, using contracts directly or other investments designed to pool money. For example, many exchange-traded funds (ETFs) are designed specifically to provide investors with a range of coverage in several assets. There are a number of ways to participate in the market. First is pure speculation, with a trade entered in the belief that value is going to move either up or down. Second is to hedge other positions; for example, if you bought shares in an oil company, you may also go short in an oil ETF; that is one example of a hedge, meaning that a loss in one position will be offset by a gain in another.

The third section of this book will explain specific futures. For now, to provide an overview of the entire futures market, the following is a list of the major commodities by type:

energy—crude oil, natural gas, coal, nuclear power, solar and wind power, electricity, ethanol

grains and oilseeds　corn, wheat, soybeans, soybean oil and meal, sugar, cotton

livestock—live cattle, feeder cattle, lean hogs, pork bellies, lumber

precious metals—gold, silver, platinum, aluminum, copper, palladium, nickel, zinc

imports and tropical products—frozen concentrated orange juice, coffee, cocoa, rice

financial futures—noncommodity contracts including those on single stocks, indices, and currencies

Another way to think about the futures market involves risk and risk transfer. The futures market not only helps anticipate the future prices of products, it also helps investors and those wanting to hedge positions transfer risks to speculators who are willing to accept those risks in exchange for profit potential. It is this risk exchange that makes futures contracts so interesting. As specific commodity prices rise and fall, corresponding action and price movement in futures contracts will react at once (when the market is open), and traders react by trading in those contracts.

The Contract and How It Works

Anyone who buys a futures contract, directly or through one of the pooled investment alternatives (like ETFs, for example) takes up a *long position*. Just as stockholders who buy shares of stock "go long," the same important definition applies to futures buyers as well. In a long position, the sequence of events is "buy, hold, sell," a well-known and common method of investing.

A *short position* is the opposite. This involves first selling a futures contract (or shares of stock) and then later closing the position with a closing purchase transaction. The sequence of events in a short position is "sell, hold, buy."

One of the most crucial elements of the contract is whether you take up a long or a short position. You can do either, and, because the market is facilitated by the futures exchanges, every short position is offset by a corresponding long position, and vice versa.

The decision to go long or short defines and distinguishes risk as well. The level of risk in short positions in futures or in any other market is usually much higher-risk than the better-known long position. Those traders who understand markets well and who are willing to accept the risk may want to sell short when they believe prices are going to move down.

Taking a short position is one way to hedge other investment positions. If you own shares of stock in a company whose price is sensitive to futures values, selling a futures contract short is one way to hedge the long stock position. Hedging can also be more complex and creative. For example, to offset a stock position, you can short an ETF for the market sector to which that company belongs.

Some traders who are involved in short positions on futures contracts (or on both long and short) are operating not as hedgers but as speculators. If they believe short-term prices are going to rise, they go long; and if they think prices will fall, they go short.

How much does a futures contract cost? The cash price of the commodity, for example, also known as the *spot price*, is defined as the current market value of the underlying commodity. The futures price is different. It is the price of a contract that anticipates future spot price levels. Futures prices tend to track spot prices, meaning that if the cost of a barrel of oil rises today, the various futures contracts for oil are going to rise too. The closest delivery month is going to be most sensitive to commodity value and how it changes, and delivery months further out will tend to change less responsively. The distinction is an important one. The spot price reflects supply and demand in the market today; futures prices are the sum of expectations about future price movement.

Another important aspect of the contract is the method by which a trade order moves through from initiation to completion. The futures exchanges are clearinghouses for execution of trades by both buyers and sellers, and supply and demand define price levels and price movements. So large exchanges, including the Chicago Board of Trade (CBOT), Chicago Mercantile Exchange (CME), and the New York Mercantile Exchange (NYMEX) contain brokers who match up each side of the transaction and ensure that the trades are made in a timely manner.

Valuable Resource: The three major futures exchanges can be found on-line, at:

Chicago Board of Trade: www.cbot.com
Chicago Mercantile Exchange: www.cme.com
New York Mercantile Exchange: www.nymex.com

All trades go through one of the exchanges. Several regional exchanges, including the Kansas City Board of Trade (www.kcbt.com) and the Minneapolis Grain Exchange (www.mgex.com), manage trades through their own brokers located on the floor of the larger national exchanges. Other, smaller futures exchanges make the trading world confusing; but it is likely that with improved Internet systems in the future, you will see mergers along the smaller exchanges or acquisitions by the larger ones. These exchanges facilitate international trading throughout the world.

When exchange members need to buy futures contracts, they present bids. Sellers present offers in the ask price. The net difference between bid and ask price is called the *spread*, and this is the profit brokers make for executing trades on the exchange floor. By definition, a bid is the highest price the buyer is willing to pay, and the ask is the lowest price a seller is willing to accept. The *floor broker* has the task of filling orders for anyone outside of the exchange, including commodity brokers, financial institutions, portfolio management companies, and the general public. Most floor brokers are excluded from trading on their own accounts.

Another type of trader is the *local*, those exchange members trading for their own accounts. These include day traders, position traders, and scalpers. A *day trader* is an individual who enters and exits positions within a single trading day, often many times. Typically, day traders limit their open positions to a few hours, and may complete their transactions within a matter of a few minutes. A *position trader* holds a futures contract open for several days or a few weeks. A *scalper* moves positions around very rapidly, often matching buyers and sellers to "scalp" the spread. Big volume equals small spreads, but a lot of small spreads can add up quickly. Scalpers provide a valuable function by matching long and short positions throughout the trading day.

Orders move from the customer, to the broker, and then to the exchange floor; from the trading floor desk, orders go directly to the trading pit to be executed. Then the process is confirmed, with information flowing back to the trading floor desk, to the exchange floor, then to the broker, and finally back to the customer. Most people tracking their trades are going to be aware of only one person, their broker, and may not realize how many steps are involved in the placement of the trade.

The Investment Value of Futures

It is a mistake to think of futures trading as an investment. By definition, investing usually involves buying a product and holding it until it grows in value, or earning current income (interest on debt securities or dividends on equities). But beyond investing is an activity known as speculation. Because futures are intangible contracts and not products, they are not investments but speculative plays. The entire futures market is a series of speculative trading decisions. The use of futures contracts as hedging strategies can certainly augment a long-term investment portfolio; but futures are not the same as tangible products like shares of stock.

Earning a profit from futures trading is more difficult than it might seem on paper. Many people have convinced themselves that by speculating on futures full time, they can retire from their jobs and make a living as traders, perhaps even get rich. The truth, however, is that this is a risky idea. You might make money on a series of consecutive trades, increasing your dollar positions each time. But it only takes one reversal to wipe out your profits. And reversals are inevitable.

Futures have to be viewed for what they are: speculative devices best used to hedge or to enter positions when you expect strong price movement in the desired direction. It also is prudent only if you limit your risks to an affordable level. Selling all your equities and mortgaging your home to begin a new venture as a futures trader is not a smart idea, even though some people in the business may promise you unimaginable riches.

A perspective on futures requires a complete appreciation of the risks involved. Those futures relating to noncommodity items, like stocks or currency exchange, can move quickly, and relative values may change in a short time. Even commodities are not intended to act as investments, but to be bought and sold on the open market. The futures contract is a method for speculating on the price of a commodity, based on changing supply and demand and based on scarcity. For example, in 2007 a movement began in the United States to develop ethanol as an alternative energy source. But as a direct consequence of farmers beginning to grow more corn, the prices of corn rose, affecting market-wide prices of many other foods as well. Corn is not held in anyone's account the way that shares of stock are held; it is grown specifically to address a demand for corn. If corn were merely to be used as feed for livestock or as a key ingredient in so many different foods, the supply and demand aspect of futures prices would be easily understood. Adding the competition between feed/food use and energy, supply and demand for corn takes on a new dimension.

This example demonstrates how a futures contract can change in value based on emerging market realities. Futures prices rise because demand also rises. For example, as China continues to grow into an industrial power, its energy demands are growing more rapidly than any other country. Oil is recognized as a finite resource, and alarming estimates are continually made about when we will run out. (Actually, since 1910, "experts" have been predicting that oil is going to run out within a decade, and these estimates are updated every decade. This topic is documented in Chapter 9 in more detail.) Demand, or at least the *perception of future de-*

mand, is what most directly affects the price of oil futures contracts. This is sensitive. For example, if conflict is anticipated in the Middle East in a way that could disrupt the flow of oil, future scarcity becomes one possibility that will affect the value of an oil futures contract.

Some esoteric factors also affect futures prices. One is inflation. Many traders expect, at the very least, that commodity values should match inflation. In other words, demand for ethanol may increase the price of corn. But even without increased demand, traders may argue that corn values (and oil, livestock, or lumber) should at least match the rate of inflation. This argument may hold during times of moderate or low inflation, but what happens when inflation rises? No one can know the answer to this, any more than they can predict future rates of inflation. Another factor is currency exchange. What happens to prices of domestic commodities *and* to imports if the U.S. dollar declines against other currencies? Concern about this causes increased speculation in U.S. and other currency futures. However, it also affects futures contract values on commodities.

The expert estimates of long-term changes are not always right, any more than expert predictions about dwindling oil reserves have been wrong for at least 100 years. Many doom-and-gloom predictions have been made concerning shortages and famines. For example, the famous Paul R. Ehrlich predicted in 1967 that between 1970 and 1985, a series of ever-worsening famines due to population growth would result from many resources running out. Not only was Ehrlich wrong about the timing of these predictions; in fact, the agri-technology of food production has improved in recent years to the extent that the threat is to the profitability of farming rather than to the ability of the human race to survive. Ehrlich's ideas led to the founding of the zero population growth movement, and he later published his predictions in book form as well.[2]

It is impossible to predict future commodity prices with certainty, just as it is impossible to predict the market value of a particular stock. Rational arguments can be made supporting the contention that prices are going to change in a particular direction, but even the most compelling arguments may be wrong. When Ehrlich predicted worldwide famine in 1967, he could not imagine how populations would actually grow nor how agriculture would change so that those people could be fed without running out of resources. Today, shortages of oil are more likely than concerns about famine nearly a half century ago.

So the "investment value" of futures cannot be defined in the same terms as the investment value of stocks or real estate. Futures contracts are going to exist for a short period of time, and they have no specific value on their own. They are predictions anticipating future value. However, a speculative value can be identified, but this is elusive. Anyone offering predictions about the future is just as likely to be wrong as a rank amateur. This fact makes futures trading very interesting. Very few futurists have ever been right about the timing or extent of events. Those predicting serious bear markets, depressions, and famines are no more likely to be right. The "science" they use is not actually science, and use of the scientific method is not useful for estimating the future. Today's global warming advocates have no actual science to prove what will happen in the future either, although many are ready to predict that higher seas and warmer climates will definitely affect commodity prices. But these proponents of the belief rely on a consensus of opinion rather than on actual data. No one really knows. And in the futures market, that equals potential for profits. Because you cannot know the price of anything in three months, the speculative futures market is the place to go to put your money down in anticipation of price direction.

A History of the Futures Market

It is worthwhile to understand how today's futures market functions, and equally interesting to see how the whole market has evolved over time. The concept of a futures contract is not a new idea.

For hundreds of years, markets have been made orderly with the use of contractual futures pricing arrangements. Without such contracts, markets would be very chaotic. For example, a farmer would have to take his grain to the marketplace and hope for the best possible price based on then-prevailing supply and demand. But with a futures market in place, speculation and hedging among traders and brokers will cover the farmers' costs of growing their crops. The same principle applies to noncommodity futures markets including stocks and indices, and currency exchange, even though a specific commodity is not being exchanged.

In the United States, a futures market began in the Midwest in the 1800s, when the geographic center of the United States was the natural region for growing crops and moving cattle. In addition, with transportation quite limited in the nineteenth century, Chicago was a natural gathering place for the markets, both east and west. As long as the United States remained primarily an agricultural society, farming and ranching commodities dominated. Even as late as 1900, the majority of U.S. citizens lived on farms or in small towns, and few people ventured more than 20 miles from their birthplace during their lifetime.

In this narrowly focused culture and economy, farmers and ranchers needed a system that would protect them from unexpected price changes between the time products were generated (crops planted or cattle processed) and taken to market. At that time, *forward contracts* were the standard. A buyer and seller could enter a forward contract on any commodity, at any time, and for any amount. It was informal and, unlike the more specific delivery dates, amounts, and prices on a formal futures market, the forward contracts of the nineteenth century lacked any market liquidity (exchangeability). As a consequence, growers often had difficulty finding a forward contract buyer.

On April 3, 1848, the first formalized commodities exchange was formed. The CBOT focused at first on forward contracts, but in 1865 this was switched out and the modern standardized futures contract became the norm. By the end of the nineteenth century, other futures exchanges were opened, including the Chicago Produce Exchange (1874, but renamed the Chicago Mercantile Exchange in 1898); and the Minneapolis Grain Exchange (1881).

In the twentieth century, the futures market expanded beyond commodity trading. In the 1970s, financial futures were introduced to speculate in futures on interest rates and currency exchange. Today's worldwide futures business includes trading of $874 trillion per year (as of 2003).[3] With Internet-based trading now possible, execution time and efficiency of information has led to record levels of volume and dollars traded.

Today's futures market is complex not only in terms of its international market, but also in what combinations of futures are traded. In the early nineteenth century, trades focused on grains used to feed farm families and to trade in rather limited markets. Exporting involved lengthy ocean shipments and international trade focused on commodities that would not spoil before reaching the market. In that century, the economic observation that "cotton is king" held true not only within the United States, but internationally as well.

For grains and grain by-products like flour, Chicago was strategically located as a future capital not only due to its proximity to farmlands and central continental site. Its access via the Great Lakes was important; and development of the Erie Canal made Chicago-based commodities easily available in New York. The Erie Canal was probably the most important transportation improvement in the history of the United States. It made commodity products available for widespread use including exports, and led to the United States becoming an economic world power. Using the same routes, immigrants and manufactured goods had easy access to the Midwest and the West. The great westward settlement movement relied greatly on movement of commodities as well as on improved transportation. So Chicago and St. Louis became key gateways for launching expansion to the Pacific territories. Without the advanced transportation systems and the orderly futures markets, this kind of expansion would have taken much longer.

The grain trade before the Civil War years was managed by a network of financial institutions, grain dealers and merchants, and buying and selling agents in clearinghouses. The use of lines of credit within this acceptance system financed farming operations, using lines of credit secured by future commodity deliveries.

On the other side of this commodity-based money market, commission agents secured warehouse receipts for quantities of grain held in storage by grain dealers. The lines of credit granted earlier were exchanged for banknotes when delivery was made from storage facilities. So in a geographically complex marketplace, a farmer in the Midwest was able to obtain payment for grains that might not be delivered in New York for many months later, all based on futures contracts and an agricultural money market.

The problem with this system was that all the companies and people involved in the transaction had to live with a lot of risk. As long as market prices remained at about the same levels, these risks were minimal. But a drought, infestation, or severe changes in demand could all spell disaster for the system; and on the financial end, a monetary panic of the type that did occur every few years also brought the interdependent system to a grinding halt.

Commercial volume increased quite a lot after 1848, the year that the Illinois-Michigan Canal was completed. This connector between the Illinois River and Lake Michigan expanded the grain market, and storage and handling technology made growth even more profitable. In the 1840s, the use of grain elevators and expanded rail lines improved the whole system, and this higher volume placed pressure on the financial side to provide a more lucrative system as well. By the 1850s, an efficient system for collecting various products, weighing, inspecting, and classifying them by quality levels emerged, making the commodities markets more efficient. The CBOT was dominant in both the shipment and financing of commodities, where merchants, bankers, and dealers also came together to resolve disputes and to form agreements.

Continued growth and expansion ultimately made it obvious that the commodities market needed a secondary market to finance the production, shipment, and sale of goods. In 1863, the CBOT formalized this market with its forward contracts and two years later, began trading futures contracts, which proved to be more efficient, more reliable, and added certainty into the markets. Given the technological limitations of railroads, telegraph communications, and hand-generated order placement, it was not until 1925 that an efficient and working clearinghouse system was in place. The original clearing procedures can be traced back to systems used at the Minneapolis Grain Exchange in 1891, but technology limited even the most efficient of systems before widespread use of telephones, not to mention air travel, automobiles, and trucks, and ultimately, computer-based order placement over the Internet.

As markets developed and expanded, so did the regulatory

structure of the industry. Up until 1920, the markets regulated themselves and the only attempted legislation was designed at shutting down these markets rather than ensuring that they operated efficiently and fairly. In 1922, the U.S. Congress passed the Grain Futures Act in response to falling grain prices after World War I. This new law required exchanges to become licensed and also set down rules for disclosures to the public.

The Commodity Exchange Act of 1936 followed a period of market reforms in the FDR era, when the Securities and Exchange Commission (SEC) was formed as part of sweeping new regulations in the stock market. The commodity law, passed in the spirit of the times and in the belief that federal oversight would prevent any future abuses, set up the Commodity Exchange Authority (CEA) as part of the Department of Agriculture. This organization monitored trading activity and was authorized to bring federal charges for price manipulation. It also limited speculation in futures by limiting positions and also regulated futures merchants. Options trading was banned on any agricultural commodities and restricted most forms of futures trading. However, the growth in commodities trading during the 1960s and 1970s made the law ineffective. It was replaced in 1974 by the Commodity Futures Trading Act, which enabled formation of the Commodity Futures Trading Commission (CFTC), which continues to act as the primary federal regulatory body to this day.

Valuable Resource: The CFTC's Web site is www.cftc.gov.

The 1974 act was modified by the Futures Trading Act of 1982. This made options legal on agricultural commodities, and clarified the jurisdictions of both the CFTC and the SEC. Most recently, Congress enacted the Commodity Futures Modernization Act in 2000, reauthorizing the CFTC for five more years and also repealing an 18-year restriction on single stock futures trading. This has opened up many permutations on the futures market, which today covers not only commodities, but precious metals, natural resources, imports, and a wide range of stock market indices, currency exchange, and interest rates.

■ **Calculating Futures Returns**

Any form of investment has to be quantified in two specific aspects: return and risk. Chapter 4 explores in detail the specific risk level of futures; for now, it is important to understand the kinds of returns you should be able to expect.

If you listen to the hype online or from telephone calls (from so-called "boiler rooms"), you can make hundreds of percent returns, but only if you act immediately. It is perplexing that anyone would agree to send a stranger $5,000 just because they were promised a $25,000 return within a matter of a few days. But it happens. You should ignore unsolicited contacts from futures dealers. As with any investment, you cannot expect to simply be given a profit just for turning over your money. That's not how profits are generated. It takes work, research, and the willingness to accept risk.

One difficulty in evaluating returns on futures contracts is that at the time a transaction is initiated, money is not exchanged. You will be required to make a deposit on margin just to ensure that you intend to either see the trade through, or close it later. The margin varies, but it may be as small as 5% of the value of the commodity. But the majority of futures business is done without cash exchange at the time you enter the contract. When you buy or sell other instruments, such as stocks, real estate, or bonds, you either pay for the entire transaction or make an arrangement for margin coverage or, in the case of real estate, for a mortgage loan for the majority of your purchase. But if you do not have to put up the money, how do you calculate your return?

This is confusing, but it works the same way as the options market in some respects. The current value of a futures contract is the agreed-upon cost of the contract, but not the future value of the underlying commodity or product. By the same rule, you can buy a stock option for a small fraction of the exercise value of stock, and later exercise or sell the option. But you are not required to exercise, so you could trade the option value of stocks worth thousands of dollars using options, and remain obligated for only a few hundred on the basis of "if and when exercised" only. The changing value of the option relies on the changing price of the stock.

The futures market is very similar. If you buy a futures contract in coffee, and the price of coffee later rises, your futures contract will be worth more as well. If coffee prices fall, so will the value of your coffee futures contract. In this contract, both buyer and seller have agreed to trade the commodity at a fixed future price, and the delivery date is well known to both sides in the transaction.

The return on a futures contract is computed in one of many ways, as it is for options. It is not realistic to base the return on the full value of a commodity as long as you are required to deposit only 5% of its future value. If you were to deposit the entire 100% value of the commodity, which is called *fully collateralized*, you would base a return on the difference in cash paid, versus cash received later when the contract was sold. But few futures traders do this, so it is not relevant to base return calculations on the full value.

One approach, which is also unrealistic for most people, is to assume an investment value you would have earned if the entire value were invested elsewhere. For example, you may use current Treasury bill yield as a comparative return, and then compare the investment value of the T-bills, versus the potential profit from buying a futures contract. This approach is valid only if you have the full amount available, and your choice is actually to fully collateralize the futures contract, or buy on margin and invest the difference. This is an academic calculation if you don't have the cash.

It is far more realistic and accurate to calculate returns from futures contracts based on the total amount placed on margin—cash at risk—plus interest, versus cash out when the position is later closed. This cash-on-cash return is going to reflect your actual return in your portfolio and, for comparative purposes, returns should always be annualized. Figure 1-1 shows the formula for annualizing returns.

For example, if you invest $450 and four months later sell for $500, your profit is $250, or 11.1%. You annualize to calculate what your return would have been if you had held the position for exactly one year. The formula:

$$\frac{11.1\%}{4} \times 12 = 33.3\%$$

FIGURE 1.1. ANNUALIZED RETURN

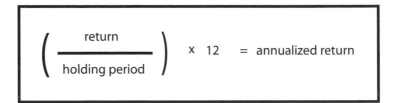

$$\left(\frac{\text{return}}{\text{holding period}} \right) \times 12 = \text{annualized return}$$

Annualizing should not be considered as a reflection of the overall return you expect to earn from any investment program. However, it is valuable as a means of comparison. When you consider potential return with risk levels in mind, an annualized basis of return calculation for several different futures strategies provides an answer. It is based on levels of risk, so the conclusion is that a given *annualized return* is possible, given the level of risk calculated to apply to a specific strategy. That is the important distinction. Of course, higher annualized returns are always possible if you are willing to accept very high risks, but you cannot compare those potential returns to lower profits on much safer strategies. So you cannot compare a 33.3% return on a long futures position to a 5% dividend on a blue chip stock, or to a 3.5% return on an insured certificate of deposit. As long as risk levels are different, you cannot fairly compare the returns.

Annualizing return is a useful tool for comparing likely outcomes for a range of futures positions, or for evaluating historical returns within your portfolio, given a series of different positions you have opened and closed. It is not reasonable to focus only on the double-digit returns and to then proclaim your genius as a futures trader (while ignoring the smaller returns and the occasional losses). That is self-deceptive, and can lead you into a false sense of success. Realistically, the real bottom line of portfolio management involves an annual assessment of outcomes. What was your beginning balance, and what was your ending balance? The difference is your annual return (adjusted for any additional deposits made throughout the year, of course). So annualized your overall portfolio provides you with a reality check each year, but granting too much weight to annualized return for a short-term position is misleading.

■ Futures Versus Stocks and Bonds

Another way to evaluate the performance of futures contracts is by comparing overall returns to those for stocks or bonds. You are likely to base your portfolio on a foundation of equities, including directly owned stocks and shares of mutual funds. If you also own shares of income funds or balanced funds, you also own debt securities. Or if you have a savings account or a CD, those also count as debt securities.

The historical equity return is normally based on the S&P 500. For debt, Treasury bonds and bills are often used as a means of comparison. Depending on the period you study, you are likely to discover a range of different outcomes between commodities, stocks, and bonds. Depending on how stocks have performed in specific time frames, commodities will either come out with better or worse returns. For this reason, long-term comparisons are really of no value as indicators of what you can expect to experience in your portfolio. The actual outcome is also going to rely on how much allocation you give to futures speculation, versus holdings of stocks and bonds. It also depends on your strategic approach. Are you simply speculating for the short term, or are you using futures contracts to hedge long positions in your portfolio?

The specific strategy you use will affect the return you should expect. If you use futures as a hedge, your intention is to reduce overall risk, so a relatively low return on futures compared to a better than average return on stocks is also deceptive. Again, if you are only speculating, the weighting factor also matters. For example, if you dedicate only 10% of your capital to futures speculation, how can you compare outcome to the 90% you leave in equity and debt? Additionally, the balance between stocks and bonds, and the balance between directly owned stocks and mutual funds, also impact your overall return.

For example, if you had bought shares in Altria, McDonald's, and ExxonMobil at the beginning of 2007 and sold all of them at the end of 2007, you would have shown impressive returns in your equity portfolio. But if you had put all your money into Citigroup and Countrywide, you would have lost more than half. So the stock portfolio return is going to be based on the decisions you made.

How can you compare this to returns from futures speculation with any degree of reliability?

The reality is that long-term historical returns are easily manipulated. Making valid comparisons of past performance is inaccurate, and depending on the date you pick, you can make the outcome look good or bad, depending on which strategy you favor. It makes more sense to acknowledge that these markets all offer potential returns, and all contain specific risks. Diversifying your portfolio to include futures contracts as speculative moves or to hedge long stock positions, is one strategy. Its outcome will rely both on timing and the degree of risk you are willing to accept.

An example of how picking the time of a comparison affects the outcome: If you compare futures to stocks between 1962 and 2006, a portfolio of futures would have outperformed the S&P 500. However, most of that positive growth took place in the 1970s. If you look instead at a range of portfolios from 1983 to 2006, stocks outperformed futures. It is impossible to believe that in the future you can somehow know when to switch from one investment to another. Just as it is impossible to time perfectly the selection of one stock over another, it is equally impossible to know when to switch in and out of stocks or futures. Looking at the past does not help, because it provides no clues about when or how similar comparisons will play out in the future.

One hint worth remembering: In times of high inflation, futures markets have historically performed better than the stock market. But looking again to the future, it is impossible to know when inflation is going to occur, how long it will last, and how severe it is going to be. The best approach is to study markets and economic trends, and attempt to hedge overall positions by anticipating inflationary times. Then futures contracts can be strategically used to hedge a stock portfolio or to speculate, selecting those futures products most likely to experience price rises if and when inflation does occur.

The next chapter moves beyond the generalized discussion of futures contracts, to describe how a trade takes place. Knowing the mechanics of trade execution is important for anyone concerned with timing in a fast-moving market.

▓ Notes

1. Ambrose Bierce, *The Devil's Dictionary*, 1911.
2. Paul R. Ehrlich, "The Population Bomb," *The New York Times,* November 4, 1970.
3. Randall Dodd, "Developing Countries Lead Growth in Global Derivatives Markets," Special Policy Brief 15, Financial Policy Forum, April 6, 2004 (www.Financialpolicy.org).

HOW FUTURES
TRADES ARE MADE

n the pre-Internet days, trading in all markets was quite primitive. The majority of people who did not have direct access to the floor of an exchange had to work with brokers. For stocks, people telephoned their stockbroker, and fees were exorbitant. For futures, people had to work with commodities brokers, and, once again, fees made this market inaccessible for most individuals.

This all began to change when stock-based discount brokers came onto the scene. In 1963, Charles Schwab began circulating a newsletter for investors, and that led to development of a new concept: low-cost brokerage services. In 1975, as the business was deregulated, it became possible for firms to compete; Schwab also was the first company to offer online brokerage services in 1996. Before that, even with discounting, investors relied on the telephone or office visits to place trades. Prices of all trading have come down substantially since the Internet became the dominant investment venue in the stock market. Prices reflect high levels of competition. In 1998, Schwab's average fee per trade was $60; by 2006, it had dropped to $14 (online trades are cheaper, but some investors continue to use the telephone to place trades, and the cost of this service is much higher).

A similar revolution has been experienced in the futures market. Before the Internet took over as a dominant market force, investors had to rely on very expensive commodities brokers, who not only charged high fees but very often provided questionable advice as well. The infamous *boiler room* was a favorite high-pressure sales organization known to telephone people and try to coerce money from them. They often targeted the elderly, and resorted to techniques such as shouting at people, making demands, and even sending couriers to their homes to pick up checks. Boiler rooms continue to exist today, but the Internet and e-mail have provided a more convenient place for boiler rooms to operate.

Another major change in the futures market—further made possible with the Internet—is the advent of indexing, in both stocks and futures. Investing in indices rather than single products has become popular with pension plans, and many people who used to invest in stocks through mutual funds and variable annuities have discovered that futures are also accessible in this way. Costs are lower than buying directly, and by relying on professional management, the risks of the futures market are of less concern. Between 2003 and 2006, investing in futures indices rose from $15 billion to $100 billion per year. During this same period, the range and specialization of indices have also expanded.

Market Diversification

Why is there a need for variation in the way you enter markets? In fact, why diversify at all? Isn't it enough to hold on to a portfolio of well-picked stocks?

The answer involves many considerations. First of all, stocks are tangible and potentially permanent, meaning you can invest and hold for many years. Futures, in comparison, are short-lived and intangible. They are speculative, and do not have any value on their own. In fact, futures contracts will rise and fall based on prices in the underlying commodity, and that is the sole driver of value in this market. However, these kinds of trades, very much like options, can enrich a stock portfolio through indices, mutual funds, and other futures-based approaches to the market.

Second, diversification spreads risk, and this aspect is a key to a well-managed portfolio. Risk is going to exist on many levels. The best known is the market risk in owning a single stock. If all your money is placed in that stock, a big decline affects your entire portfolio. However, risk also may apply to an entire sector like energy or banking, so even a stock portfolio should spread out among many sectors. But there is also a market-wide risk. If the stock market undergoes a long-term bear trend, a majority of stocks are going to fall with market averages.

A solution to this risk is diversification between dissimilar markets, and this is where futures can provide a valuable form of protection. You have probably realized the value in diversifying between equity (stocks or real estate) and debt (bonds or income mutual funds). A problem with diversifying with real estate is the illiquidity of direct ownership, which accounts for the popularity of mortgage pools, real estate sector mutual funds, and real estate investment trusts. A similar convenience is found in futures index investing, which enables you to diversify broadly into markets rather than buying an entire range of a product, or all of the stocks in a stock market index. For example, you can easily buy shares in the S&P 500 as an alternative to buying small portions of each of the 500 companies in that index.

Comparing today's futures market to that of the past points out how much more flexibility you have today. In fact, the traditional risks of owning commodities have been virtually eliminated through the use of indices and mutual funds. The most obvious is price risk, or the risk that price will change in a direction creating a loss instead of a profit. But futures are also sensitive to risk from outside influences. Political unrest in the Middle East affects the price of oil in the United States and elsewhere. The increased demand for ethanol makes the price of corn rise, which further affects feed costs for livestock. So isolated and singular events can have a rippling affect in the futures market. The importance of diversification in its obvious forms is fairly well understood. In the futures market, it is equally important to be aware of how events— political, economic, and market—affect prices of seemingly unrelated commodities and economic futures (interest rates and currency values, for example).

Before the development of practical and convenient vehicles

like indices and futures mutual funds, hapless individual investors simply were left out of the market. Diversification was limited or had to be achieved via traditional vehicles (savings accounts, stocks, directly owned real estate, and mutual funds). Hedging as a strategic move was not generally available for individual investors. The options market, in which hedging is today both practical and affordable, also was expensive when you had to rely on a broker. The commission costs were so high that you needed substantial movement in option premium just to break even, so any diversification involving options was limited to pure speculation or covered call writing.

These forms of diversification are valuable and workable, and even before low-cost transactions were available, often made sense. But the point is diversification was a very restricted activity. Pre-Internet systems were not only slow and expensive, they also lacked the "internal diversification" that makes indices and funds so attractive. This concept—*internal diversification*—refers to the spreading of risk within an index or fund itself. Today, you do not have to trade directly in commodities, even though some traders do just that. This activity should be reserved only for the most experienced speculator or hedger, whereas most individual investors will be content with a more passive approach.

"Risk" in commodity investing used to include price risk, meaning that even if a trade were profitable, the transaction cost going in and coming out made it impractical, or resulted in a net loss. By investing through pooled vehicles, you avoid this price risk while also achieving very effective levels of internal diversification.

Commodities Indices

Popular commodity indices include several major selections. The Goldman Sachs Commodity Index (GSCI) contains over $50 billion in investor dollars. As of December 18, 2007, weighting included 73% in energy, 7% industrial metals, 2% precious metals, 14% agriculture, and 4% livestock. Figure 2.1 shows this breakdown.

Valuable Resource: To find the current weighting of the GSCI, go to www2 .goldmansachs.com/gsci/insert.html.

FIGURE 2.1. GSCI WEIGHTING

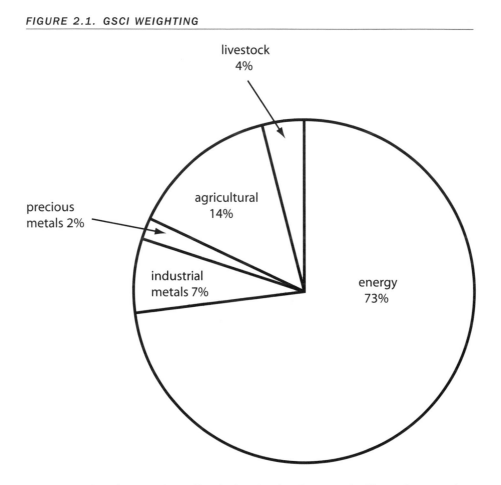

Another commodity index is the Reuters/Jeffries Commodity Research Bureau Index, more commonly referred to as the Reuters/CRB Index. This index includes energy 17.6%, grains and oilseeds 17.6%, copper and cotton 17.6%, livestock 12%, precious metals 17.6%, and imports 17.6%. Figure 2.2 shows this breakdown.

A third choice is the Rogers International Commodities Index (RICI). This index includes only commodities that are involved in international trade, and excludes those used primarily for national consumption. Table 2.1 summarizes the initial weighting of components as reported in the *2007 RCI Handbook*.

Also check Figure 2.3 for a visual breakdown of these major components.

FIGURE 2.2. REUTERS/JEFFRIES WEIGHTING

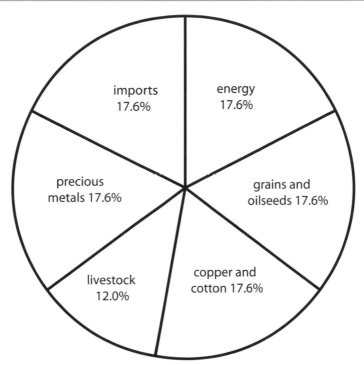

Valuable Resource: For more details on RICI or to view the latest handbook, go to www.diapasoncm.com/indices/pdf/RICI_Index_Manual.pdf.

Another is the S&P Commodity Index, which was first introduced in 2000. This is called the "Geometric Series" and measures a cross-section of commodities offering active U.S. futures contracts. The index includes five sectors—energy, metals, grains, livestock, and fibers or imports.

As of 2006, the index included natural gas 18%, unleaded gas 12%, heating oil 12%, crude oil 11%, wheat 5%, live cattle 5%, and the remaining 37% spread among futures with less than 5% of the total. Figure 2.4 provides a visual breakdown.

Valuable Resource: Find out more about the S&P Commodity Index at www2.standardandpoors.com.

The Dow Jones-AIG Commodity Index is one of the most popular indices in the futures market. No component class is allowed

TABLE 2.1. RICI INITIAL WEIGHTING

Commodity	Weight	Commodity	Weight
Crude Oil	21.00%	Soybean Oil	2.00%
Brent Crude Oil	14.00	Sugar	2.00
Wheat	7.00	Platinum	1.80
Corn	4.75	Lean Hogs	1.00
Aluminum	4.00	Cocoa	1.00
Copper	4.00	Nickel	1.00
Cotton	4.05	Tin	1.00
Heating Oil	1.80	Rubber	1.00
Gas Oil	1.20	Lumber	1.00
RBOB Gasoline	3.00	Soybean Meal	0.75
Natural Gas	3.00	Canola	0.67
Soybeans	3.00	Orange Juice	0.66
Gold	3.00	Rice	0.50
Live Cattle	2.00	Oats	0.50
Coffee	2.00	Azuki Beans	0.50
Zinc	2.00	Palladium	0.30
Silver	2.00	Barley	0.27
Lead	2.00	Greasy Wool	0.25
		Total	100.00%

Source: *2007 RICI Handbook.*

to account for more than 33% of the total weighting in the index, and no single commodity is allowed to make up more than 2% of the overall index. As of January 2007, the index included petroleum 20%, natural gas 13%, grains 18%, vegetable oils 3%, livestock 9%, precious metals 9%, industrial metals 19%, and imports (these are called "softs") 9%. See Figure 2.5.

Valuable Resource: For more about the Dow Jones-AIG Commodity Index, go to www.djindexes.com/mdsidx/index.cfm?event = showAi glntro.

The Deutsche Bank Liquid Commodity Index, originated in 2003, follows only six commodity contracts: two each among energy, metals, and agricultural sectors. These are light sweet crude oil 35%, heating oil 20%, gold 10%, aluminum 12.5%, corn 11.25%, and wheat 11.25%. See Figure 2.6.

FIGURE 2.3. RICI WEIGHTING

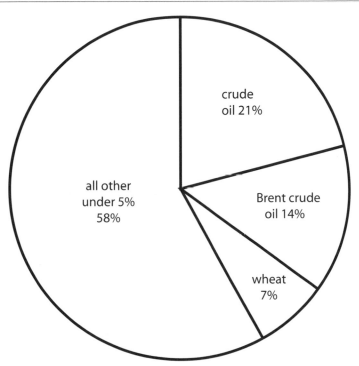

Valuable Resource: Deutsche Bank's Web page is dbfunds.db.com.

These are *tracking funds,* which are designed not to own the commodities or even the futures contracts. Investors can use the indices in several ways:

1. *Benchmarks.* Institutions often use tracking indices to compare the performance of their own portfolios. As a measurement for a diversified portfolio of stocks and bonds, these portfolio managers want to ensure that their holdings match or perform better than the tracking index. As an individual, you can use a commodity index in the same way, comparing your portfolio's performance to the separate index outcome. Many people use stock indices in the same way, although this is not really accurate. For example, you might observe that today, the Dow Jones Industrial Average (DJIA) rose 45 points, but your portfolio rose $75 net. This is not accurate, because the index is point-based and

FIGURE 2.4. S&P COMMODITY INDEX WEIGHTING

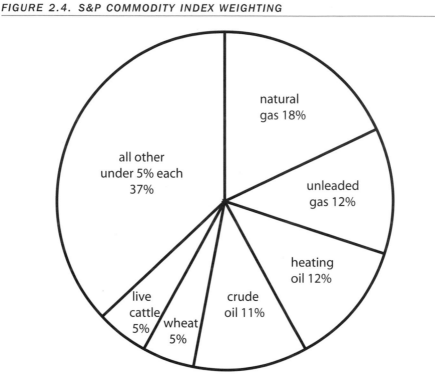

weighted; and your portfolio's performance depends on the mix
of holdings. So while the DJIA may provide a directional indicator, it is not accurate to compare points to dollars. In comparison, the year-to-year performance of a commodity tracking
index does indicate the relative strength or weakness of the
economy.

2. *Investment via replication.* You may also refer to a tracking fund
   and replicate its commodity breakdown (or parts of it) by investing in the same contracts. For example, if you note that most
   of the large indices emphasize energy over most other commodities, you may decide to also buy energy futures contracts for
   your portfolio; or to enter into the energy market through another method (such as buying stocks or shares of an ETF).

3. *Indicator only.* As a method for deciding whether or not to invest in stocks or other market segments, you can use commodity indices as economic indicators. Some analysts believe that

FIGURE 2.5. DOW JONES-AIG COMMODITY INDEX WEIGHTING

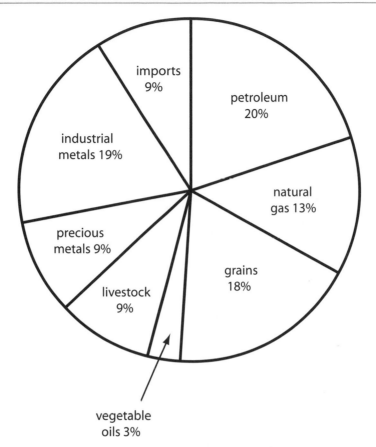

commodity prices anticipate the direction of the economy at large, and that economic trends anticipate stock market trends as well. In times when prices are rising, analysts expect stocks to follow; and vice versa, when commodity prices fall, the belief is that stocks will also fall.

4. *Direct ownership of the futures contract.* You can open a futures account directly and purchase futures contracts based on commodity tracking index breakdowns or for part of the commodity breakdown. This is going to be difficult if you plan to duplicate the entire tracking range of commodities, however, and alternative methods are more practical.

FIGURE 2.6. DEUTSCHE BANK COMMODITY INDEX WEIGHTING

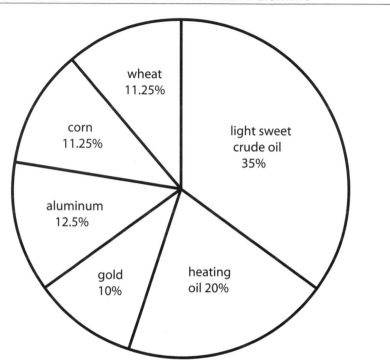

5. *Buying futures contracts of the index itself.* Some indices market tracking contracts, which enable you to trade in the entire portfolio of the index. This is a very practical method for duplicating the range of contracts, but without needing to trade each and every one directly.

6. *Exchange-traded funds (ETFs).* The relatively new ETF market provides great flexibility for investors, letting you enter a range of markets with instant diversification. You can own shares of an ETF without the cost or risk of buying commodities directly; in fact, you can even sell short shares of an ETF, and many even allow you to write options. Thus, you can write options on a basket of futures contracts, an idea that is appealing to those recognizing the potential but unwilling to take the risk of going short on individual futures contracts. You can also trade commodity ETF shares the same way you trade stocks, for very low cost, using your online brokerage account. Deutsche Bank, which trades on the American Stock Exchange (symbol DBC),

offered the first commodity ETF in 2006. In the 12-month period through December 2007, this ETF earned more than a 20% return. You can trade this fund through your online brokerage account, and it replicates the Deutsche Bank Liquid Commodity Index described previously.

Expect the range of commodity-based ETFs to continue growing in the future. As of the end of 2007, other commodity ETFs include:

U.S. Oil Fund (AMEX: USO)

streetTRACKS Gold Shares (AMEX: GLD)

iShares Silver Trust (AMEX: SLV)

JPMorgan Commodity Curve Index (NYSE: JPMCCI)

PowerShares Agriculture Fund (AMEX: DBA)

PowerShares DB Oil Fund (AMEX: DBO)

PowerShares Silver Fund (AMEX: DBS)

There is a lot to choose from; but how do you know which indices are appropriate for you, and which are not? Regardless of how you use these indices or decide to enter the market, you need to be able to compare and analyze the index. You can find pertinent information in the literature provided by each index. You should include the following four areas of testing in your comparative analysis:

1. *Rolling method employed.* The commodity indices merely track performance of futures contracts, and are not set up to take delivery. So as a delivery date approaches, the index *rolls* its contracts, replacing the current one with the next, known as the *front month contract*. The roll generates a yield, based on price differences between current contract and the one rolled, which is going to be worth more (due to the greater amount of time to delivery date). Policies on frequency of rolling vary, and these policies affect yield.

2. *Weighting calculations.* The method an index uses to weight the

futures it tracks varies as well. Some indices use a *production-weighted* method, providing greater weight to those commodities based on its level of worldwide production. Others follow a *component weighting* method, calculated on the liquidity level in futures trading. In addition, some indices adjust their weighting periodically, while others make changes on a continuing basis.

3. *Components of the index.* How does the index determine what to include? This varies, with some basing their tracking on *production value* and others on *liquidity* or volume of trading activity.

4. *Rebalancing frequency.* The components are rarely left intact in one configuration indefinitely. The actual components and their weighting levels are subject to adjustment, so that the index remains representative of the mix of futures contracts that it tracks. The frequency of this review can determine how out of date an index might be, and how long it will be before rebalancing occurs.

Futures Merchants, Advisors, Operators

Perhaps the easiest, most flexible, and most affordable method for entering the futures market is through one of the ETFs based on a tracking index. This method, accomplished through an online broker in the same manner as buying and selling stocks, is instant, cheap, and relatively safe (at least as safe as trading in stocks, and certainly far safer than buying futures contracts directly). In its brief history, the commodity ETF market, as a whole, has been more volatile than the stock market. However, this may reflect actual movement in commodity values more than any inherent tendency toward volatility.

One drawback to the ETF approach is that you need to find a venue that closely matches what you are seeking. You may not be able to get an exact match. A recurring criticism of ETFs for not only commodities, but stocks and sectors as well, is that the net return tends to be an average of all the components in the basket. The question is raised, Why not buy the best-performing members of the basket rather than the whole thing? This is a good idea, as long as you can be assured that you pick the best-performing component in the future. For many traders, the ETF route limits risk, but it also limits the opportunity to outperform the market. For these less risk-averse traders, there are three designations for buying or selling futures contracts directly; the Commodity Futures Trading Commission, which was formed in 1974 and operates under the Futures Modernization Act of 2000, regulates all of these designations.

Valuable Resource: For more information about the CFTC, go to the agency's Web site at www.cftc.gov.

The three regulated commodities designations are:

1. *The Commodity Trading Advisor (CTA)* manages traders' accounts and maintains detailed records. Disclosure reports have to be filed periodically with the National Futures Association (NFA), which is the industry's regulatory body. The CTA acts as a combination of facilitator and advisor to those wanting to trade individually in futures contracts.

Valuable Resource: To find out more about the NFA, go to www.nfa .futures.org.

2. *A Futures Commission Merchant (FCM)* is licensed to accept and to solicit orders for futures trades, and may also grant credit to customers, including individuals and brokerage houses through which investors enter transaction orders. The FCM is required to file monthly financial reports with the Division of Clearing and Intermediary Oversight, part of the CFTC.

3. *A Commodity Pool Operator (CPO)* acts as a trading pool for many individuals or companies. The CPO does not have to register directly, but must distribute a disclosure document to clients, send out account statements, and present audited financial statements. The CPO also must maintain detailed records of transactions and pool operations, including any transactions made by pool officers. The disclosure documents and annual financial statements are filed with the NFA. In many respects,

the CPO operates like stock-based mutual funds, while it is also possible for investors to trade in commodities through traditional funds and ETFs. The traditional mutual funds involved with commodities rely on professional management to select futures contracts, so they differ from the commodity indices and their tracking funds, as well as ETFs, which identify a basket of futures in advance. The traditional mutual funds specializing in commodities include Pimco's Commodity Real Return Fund (www.pimco.com) and the Oppenheimer Real Asset Fund (www.oppenheimerfunds.com). Because these are traditional funds, shares have to be bought directly from management and cannot be traded through brokerage accounts.

Publicly Traded Companies and Partnerships

One way to view the entire futures business is to take a broader economic view. The futures market does represent the health and trend of the U.S. economy in many respects. Because it involves commodities of all kinds as well as major financial futures (including futures on stocks and stock market indices), virtually every aspect of economic growth and commerce is represented in futures trading.

Even so, this does not mean it is necessary to use futures contracts to take part in this broader economic trend. You can very narrowly focus your attention through the stock market as well, using futures trends as a benchmark. For example, if you conclude that the energy sector is going to grow substantially over the next few months or years, you can invest in the commodity itself, including many variations of energy; or you could buy individual energy sector stocks or even a stock market ETF or energy sector index. You can also buy futures on individual stocks, an idea explained in a later chapter; or use options to leverage capital and control blocks of energy company stocks.

When you buy publicly traded company stock, you earn dividends as long as you own shares; and capital gains when you sell. You can further use options to create additional cash income through covered call writing, and you can offset stock positions by hedging in the futures market for the sector. Most analysts studying both stocks and futures trading have noticed the relationship between the two. The trends do appear to cross market lines, meaning, for example, that as energy prices rise and futures contracts also follow the price trend, the stock energy sector also tends to benefit in the same direction. As a result, buying energy stocks or sector index shares is yet another way to invest in the energy commodity. If you are bearish on a particular futures contract, you may hesitate to go short in the contract itself, and you might be equally worried about selling short energy stocks. An alternative is to go long on put options. Although this is a low-risk move as a long position, it is also a bearish position on the stock or sector.

There are many ways to play the futures market other than taking risks directly. The combination of mutual funds, ETFs, commodity indices, and even stock or sector plays including options present you with a vast array of choices.

Chapter 3 moves the discussion forward by explaining how to read and interpret the listings you find in the financial press or online. Futures listings are difficult to read for novices, especially if you are accustomed to the relatively simple and straightforward listings for stocks.

C H A P T E R   3

READING FUTURES PRICES

Futures prices are difficult to read for one primary reason: Not all of them are in the same unit increments. On the stock market, you are accustomed to seeing share prices quoted in dollars and cents for virtually every stock available; but in the futures market, there are many different value increments, as well as varying minimum contract sizes.

▪ The Basic Futures Quotation

Contracts trade under a two-part alphabetical system. First is the one- or two-digit designation for each type of futures contract; second is the delivery month. The symbols for each type of commodity used in this book are:

light sweet crude oil	CL	frozen concentrated	
unleaded gas	HU	orange juice (FCOJ)	OJ
heating oil	HO	sugar	SB
natural gas	NG	corn	C
cocoa	CC	wheat	W
coffee	KC	oats	O
cotton	CT	soybeans	S

soybean meal	SM	silver	SI
soybean oil	BO	platinum	PL
copper	HG	live cattle	LC
aluminum	AL	feeder cattle	FC
lumber	LB	frozen pork bellies	PB
gold	GC	lean hogs	LH

Delivery months used in contract quotations are:

January	F	July	N
February	G	August	Q
March	H	September	U
April	J	October	V
May	K	November	X
June	M	December	Z

So the February contract for light sweet crude is reported as CLG, for example. When a commodity trades on more than one exchange, the symbol will be different as well. So it is important to ensure that the symbol you refer to matches with the exchange where you expect it to trade.

There are two popular methods for reporting current futures prices. First is limited to the contract that is of greatest trading interest. This is usually the contract whose delivery date is second in line. For example, in the month of December, the December contract is about to expire, so most of the "action" is going to be on the March contract. If you see a listing with a single futures contract, it is usually this second-in-line delivery date.

Another method, which more accurately portrays the range of market pricing for a particular grouping of futures, shows all the contracts over the coming year and, often, over a longer period. You may see as many as 10 or 12 different delivery dates, but volume is going to focus on the second and third in line. Thus, in December, the March and June (or April and July) contracts will have the highest trading volume. Actual delivery months vary by commodity, so this adds to the confusion, much as the options market, which also trades on three separate calendar cycles. Unlike options, which always adhere to a three-month expiration cycle, some commodities trade on a monthly series, such as 12 consecutive months and 12 delivery dates.

The single-delivery date quotation may vary from one financial newspaper or online site to another, but at the very least, it will contain:

- The type of commodity, its exchange, and trading increment
- Delivery month
- Opening price for the latest day
- High price for the latest day
- Low price for the latest day
- Closing price
- Change from previous close
- Trading volume
- Prior settlement price
- Open interest (number of contracts)

Figure 3-1 summarizes a typical futures quotation for live cattle.

This listing reflects prices on the CME, an important distinction. Many commodities trade on more than one exchange. Also in the heading is the definition of contract size and denomination of

FIGURE 3.1. FUTURES LISTING, SINGLE LINE REPORT

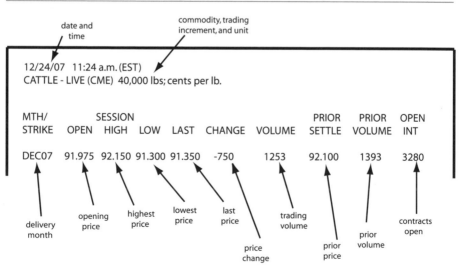

the prices that follow. In the case of live cattle futures, the futures contract size is 40,000 pounds and the prices are shown in cents per pound.

The second way that futures contracts are reported is with a listing of all current contracts available. While the information is identical as that for a single delivery date, it is more revealing when you can view all the contracts together. Figure 3-2 gives an example.

Notice how the volume and open interest change from one delivery date to another. The greatest volume is normally found in the second delivery date; in this case, December remains open, but February—the second delivery date—reports the greatest level of open interest and volume of trading. This is because commodity indices and ETFs (as well as individual traders) roll out of current contracts to avoid the delivery strike, and into the next contract. Because of the continual rolling effect, the tendency is for volume and open interest to jump between the soonest and next dates; and to then taper off throughout the remaining delivery dates.

Each futures contract trades in increments unique to its nature. Live cattle has a trading schedule every other month: February, April, June, August, October, and December. Some trade quarterly or over 12 consecutive months.

FIGURE 3.2. FUTURES LISTING, MULTIPLE LINE REPORT

12/24/07 11:24 a.m. (EST)
CATTLE - LIVE (CME) 40,000 lbs; cents per lb.

MTH/ STRIKE	SESSION OPEN	HIGH	LOW	LAST	CHANGE	VOLUME	PRIOR SETTLE	PRIOR VOLUME	OPEN INT
DEC07	91.975	92.150	91.300	91.350	−750	1253	92.100	1393	3280
FEB08	95.200	95.350	94.925	94.975	−550	5124	95.525	6492	122760
APR08	97.100	97.200	96.825	96.900	−700	3517	97.600	4707	63470
JUN08	93.600	94.000	93.400	93.550	−825	1183	94.375	3525	22887
AUG08	94.900	95.350	94.800	95.000	−725	686	95.725	1520	15524
OCT08	99.100	99.200	98.900	99.050	−575	174	99.625	492	6025
DEC08	99.650	99.650	99.200	99.500	−125	18	99.625	129	4192
FEB09	100.500	100.800	100.500	100.500	UNCH	6	100.500	60	1522
APR09	100.000	100.000	100.000	100.000	UNCH	1	100.000	8	235

Futures Contract Unit Definitions

The volume or weight of a commodity is going to vary by the commodity itself, and the unit of cost used is not the same for all. You need to know some important definitions before getting into the specific unit distinctions. In addition, it is important to recognize that with a variety of different commodities on the market, the unit size varies because of some very basic differences. Some are solid, others liquid or gas in form; some are going to be valued by weight, others by volume. And volume valuation means that different agricultural commodities are not going to have the same weight either, so a volume unit size may involve different weight. Precious metals are valued in price per ounce, whereas other commodities come in price per pound or ton.

In the energy market, you will hear about various kinds of oil or gas. Crude oil is highly explosive and flammable and is not commonly used in the form in which it comes out of the ground. Refining is the process by which crude oil is turned into gas, diesel gas, asphalt, heating oil, kerosene, and liquid petroleum gas. This is done by distillation, based on different boiling points for each product. By-products also are used to manufacture plastics, solvents, detergent, and some fibers (nylon and polyesters). Because there are many varieties of crude oil, specific and popularly cited types show up as separate commodities listings.

Reformulated Blendstock for Oxygenate Blending (RBOB) is unleaded gasoline futures, which sell in increments of 42,000 gallons (1,000 barrels). Light sweet crude (containing low viscosity and low sulfur) is the most liquid form of crude oil, which is refined and processed into many different grades. Brent crude comes from Shell UK Exploration's North Sea oil fields. Exploration companies have followed the practice of naming oil fields after birds, and in this case, the field is named for the brent goose. Natural gas is measured in MMBTUs. The MM is Roman numeral for "a thousand thousand," or one million; BTUs are for British Thermal Units. One BTU represents the amount of energy needed to increase the temperature of one pint of water by one degree Fahrenheit.

In other types of commodities, weights and measurements vary by name and type. Industrial metals futures are reported in metric tons (MT), which are 1,000 kilograms or about 2,205 pounds. A troy ounce, used for precious metals futures, is equal to 1/12 pound. In comparison, most people who cook are more familiar with the avoirdupois ounce, which is 1/16 pound.

Lumber is measured in board feet. One board foot is equal to a piece of wood measuring one foot long, by one foot across, by one inch of depth (1' × 1' × 1").

Many agricultural and livestock futures are measured in pounds. A pound is denoted as *lb.*, which is derived from the Latin *libra*, the zodiacal sign shown with scales representing balance.

Other agricultural futures are reported in bushels. A bushel is a dry measurement of mass, and depending on the commodity, weight is going to vary. One bushel is equal to 2,150.42 cubic inches, and there are four pecks per bushel.

Futures for financial instruments are measured in percentages (interest rates), or currency units (dollars, Euros, pounds); and financial futures for stocks or indices are reported in dollar value or index point values.

Table 3-1 provides a summary of the most common commodities and their units of measurement in futures contracts.

Reading Futures Charts

Price charts for futures contracts are similar to stock price charts in many important respects. Both show price movement over time and both use a charting format familiar to most stock market investors or analysts.

Figure 3-3 shows a four-month daily chart for live cattle futures that expired in December 2007. The chart shows price trends as of December 24, 2007. Volume of trades is shown at the bottom. Note how volume falls off to nearly zero as the delivery date approaches.

Prices fell over this period. In comparison, prices for Brent crude oil futures rose, as Figure 3-4 shows. This is a December 2007 chart for the contract expiring in February 2008. In this instance, volume remained high because the December contract

TABLE 3.1. COMMODITY UNITS

Commodity	Unit	Commodity	Unit
Light Sweet Crude Oil	barrels	Lumber	b.f.
Unleaded Gas	gallons		
Heating Oil	gallons	Copper	MTs
Natural Gas	MMBTUs	Lead	MTs
		Nickel	MTs
Cocoa	MTs	Zinc	MTs
Coffee	lbs.	Aluminum	MTs
Cotton	lbs.		
Frozen Concentrated		Silver	t.oz.
Orange Juice (FCOJ)	lbs.	Platinum	t.oz.
Sugar	lbs.	Gold	t.oz.
Corn	bushels		
Wheat	bushels	Lean Hogs	lbs.
Oats	bushels	Live Cattle	lbs.
Soybeans	bushels	Feeder Cattle	lbs.
Soybean Meal	tons	Frozen Pork Bellies	lbs.
Soybean Oil	lbs.		

lbs.   pounds
MMBTUs million British Thermal Units
MTs   metric tons
t.oz.   troy ounces
b.f.   board feet

rolled over to February. This contract was where most of the trading action and open interest were focused at the time.

For the live cattle contract, the price and volume trend was predictable because delivery date was so close. Volume and open interest also fell as the December delivery date approached. In virtually all futures contracts, proximity of delivery date causes this to occur, because those with positions roll them forward. So the activity in December contracts declines as those positions are closed and replaced with the next-occurring delivery date.

On both of these charts, the section immediately below price shows trends in the oscillator known as "moving average convergence/divergence," or MACD. This is a popular measurement of buy and sell trends, intended to anticipate momentum in either direction. Two moving averages are calculated (in futures, these are

FIGURE 3.3. LIVE CATTLE—DECEMBER 7 CONTRACT

Source: Charts provided courtesy of TradingCharts.com: http://futures.tradingcharts.com; created with SuperCharts by Omega Research © 1997.

usually 26-day and 12-day averages). MACD is the difference between the two, and the trend itself is measurement of convergence (the two averages moving closer together) or divergence (moving apart).

Technicians contend that when MACD falls below a signal line (0.00), it creates a sell signal; and when it moves above, that creates a buy signal. As the trend moves across the signal line, it is called a crossover point. In the first chart for live cattle, MACD was well above the signal line in August, but it approached the line at the October price peak and then declined below. Prices did fall after that point, partially reacting to the MACD trend, and partly due to rolling as the delivery date approached. The Brent crude oil futures contract showed MACD trends well above the line beginning in October and continuing into the delivery month.

MACD also implies when a futures contract is overbought or oversold. When the shorter-term moving average diverges from the longer-term (when MACD rises), it becomes likely that the price

FIGURE 3.4. BRENT CRUDE OIL—FEBRUARY 2008 CONTRACT

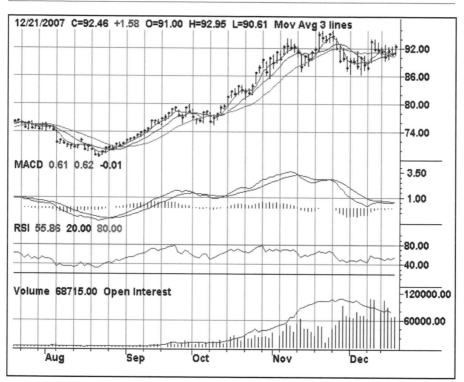

Source: Charts provided courtesy of TradingCharts.com: http://futures.tradingcharts.com; created with SuperCharts by Omega Research © 1997.

is overbought and will retreat. On declines, the oversold indicator presents the opposite scenario.

When MACD moves significantly above or below the futures contract price (when it diverges), it anticipates a price reversal. Thus, if the MACD is below the daily price line, that implies that prices are going to fall in the short term. This bearish divergence is equivalent to an oversold condition, but is more likely to be spotted in the moving average lines overlaying daily price trends, than in the MACD line itself.

Beneath the MACD is a second technical indicator, labeled RSI. This is the Relative Strength Index, a momentum indicator based on price trends. It measures the strength of the current price trend, in comparison to the former trend itself. The line is calculated by comparing differences in daily closing prices and then calculating an average. Thanks to the speed and convenience of online free charts, you do not need to perform the calculation by hand. Like moving averages, you can avoid the complexities of the math by simply going to one of the sites that provide free charting.

Valuable Resource: One of the many sites offering free futures contract charts is www.futures.tradingcharts.com.

When you see RSI above 70, it suggests that current price levels are overbought. The live cattle chart only went above 70 in its earlier period, August 2007. The Brent crude oil also went above this level briefly, in September and October. As you can see, the indicator did seem to anticipate downward price movements for the live cattle contract; but in the case of Brent crude oil, the trend was short-lived and preceded upward price movement. This inconsistency points out an important aspect of technical analysis: All indicators imply trends but don't prove them, and any interpretation should be done in conjunction with a range of different attributes.

The RSI is expected to remain between 40 and 80 in most conditions. When it falls below 40, it indicates an oversold condition. The cattle futures contract did not fall below that level until delivery date was quite close. The Brent contract briefly touched that level early on but, like its later trend, the level held too briefly to serve as a strong indicator. RIS is a measure of the strength in a trend, and should not be used as a specific buy or sell signal by itself.

RSI can also be used as a way to measure a form of divergence. For example, when prices move higher but RSI does not move as you would expect, it could indicate weakness in the price trend. Generally, as prices rise, you would expect RSI to track. When it does not track over 20 or more days, it anticipates a pending price reversal. The same works in reverse. When prices fall, RSI should follow as well, at least until price becomes oversold. But if RSI remains steady or rises, it indicates that the apparent price trend is weak and will not continue.

Both MACD and RSI are technical indicators, and some traders place more importance on them than others. Some highly detailed analysis may be involved for the true believer in technical analysis; but in practice, it makes sense to use indicators such as these as *part* of a broader program of analysis. That should involve moving average and price comparisons and some strong fundamentals, such as worldwide and domestic supply and demand indicators. For example, if political tensions in the Middle East are becoming worse, that could easily cause oil prices to rise. If a new, massive oil field is discovered in the United States, or refinery capacity increases, that may cause oil futures prices to fall. The point is you can use many different indicators to track future prices and to anticipate upcoming price direction. The technical and chart-based patterns of price are valuable, but they are only aspects to a broader trend.

Types of Charts

The charts in the previous section show the range of trading in each day, represented by the daily vertical bar. The high side is the highest price reached on that day, and the low side is the lowest. The smaller vertical bars for each day, called ticks, show the day's opening price (on the left) and closing price (on the right). This format is called the OHLC ("open, high, low, close") chart. If moving averages are also used on the chart, it is seen as a line moving through the series of daily bars. Figure 3-5 summarizes the features of the OHLC chart.

Another way that price reporting occurs is with the candlestick chart. On this version, the open, high, low, and close prices are also shown; but the *direction* of price movement is also shown, using a rectangular bar. A black bar indicates a downward price movement for the day, and a white bar is used for upward-moving price trends. Figure 3-6 shows the features of a candlestick bar.

The candlestick chart looks somewhat different than the more familiar OHLC. Referring back to Figure 3-5, which was an OHLC chart, the same chart using candlesticks looks like the version shown in Figure 3-7.

You can tell at a glance where trends have evolved with the candlestick chart. A series of black rectangles represents a downtrend, and a series of white or clear rectangles points the way to an uptrend. For this visual advantage, candlestick charts are popular for futures charting as well as for stocks. Figure 3-8 shows the

FIGURE 3.5. OHLC CHART

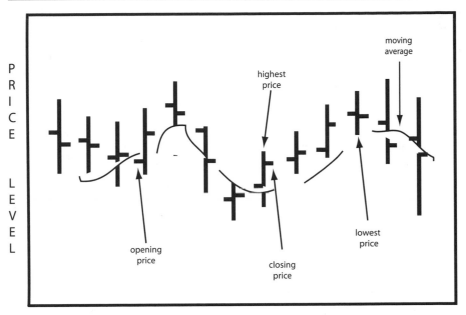

FIGURE 3.6. CANDLESTICK FORMATIONS

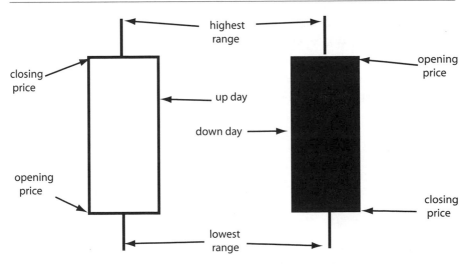

FIGURE 3.7. CANDLESTICK CHART

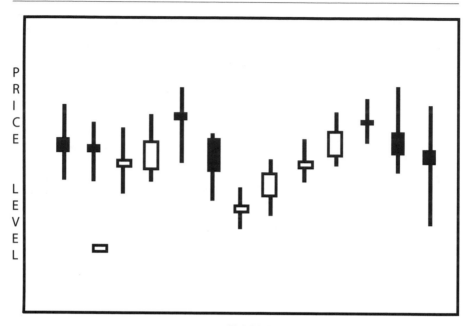

TIME

wheat futures contract for March 2008 as of late December 2007 in OHCL format, and Figure 3-9 shows it in candlestick format.

The next chapter moves beyond the methods for accessing price, and explores the broader question of *risk*. Every investor and trader should be interested in defining various kinds of risk before placing money into a market. Futures risk is not the same as the risks in stocks or other markets.

FIGURE 3.8. WHEAT—MARCH 2008 CONTRACT

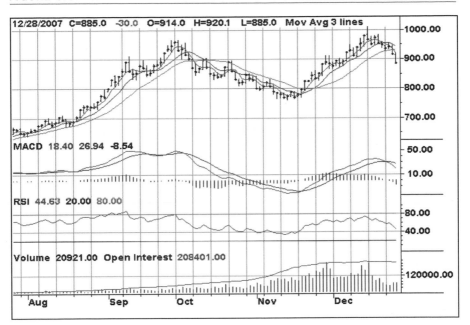

Source: Charts provided courtesy of TradingCharts.com: http://futures.tradingcharts.com; created with SuperCharts by Omega Research © 1997.

FIGURE 3.9. WHEAT—MARCH 2008 CONTRACT

Source: Charts provided courtesy of TradingCharts.com: http://futures.tradingcharts.com; created with SuperCharts by Omega Research © 1997.

| | | | | | | | June | 111-087 111 |
| | 3.2076 | -.003? | 66,509 | Sept | 113-185 110 |

MBL.					3D Day Federal Fund.
3.0307	-.0230	19.962	2 Yr. Treasury Note
3.0217	-.0250	98.575	June	106-007 106-0
MMBL.				3D Day Federal Fund.
11.280	312	15,673	April	97,735 97.7
11.329	128	140.673	May	97,925 97.96
11.452	212	81,584		1 Month Libor (CME)-$
1.589	180	66.643	May	97,2100 97.230
364	160	55.727	June	97.2850 97.2950
128	180	43.819		Eurodollar (CME)-$1,000.0
			May	97,1450 97.1925
			June	97.1200 97.2150
22.75	104,583	Sept	97,0400 97.1500
22.75	567,041	Dec	96.8600 96.9700
03	191	**Currency Futures**

RISK LEVELS OF FUTURES

Risk appears to be such a basic concept that many investors and traders overlook it. Identifying a portfolio as "diversified" does not necessarily mean that it is; and when people call themselves "conservative" but then speculate wildly on long shots, it makes the point: Truly understanding risk requires a sincere effort to match personal risk tolerance and investing goals with a range of appropriate products.

Investors who analyze risk know that:

1. *There is an important difference between investing and trading.* The investor tends to buy stocks and other products with the idea of holding those positions open for some period of time. That may be weeks or months, but more likely it is years. Those who buy real estate invest for the long term, defined as five years or more, perhaps the remainder of a person's life. Stockholders may be "value investors," meaning they seek well managed, superior companies available at a discount, buy stock, and hold for the long term. Some value investment experts suggest buying such stocks and then forgetting about them for many years. This may not be wise because, increasingly, market and

company-specific status changes rapidly in the global economy and the Internet age. Some other investors seek "growth stocks," which are generally thought to be those most likely to outpace the market as a whole and produce superior returns.

Investors tend to be more conservative than traders. If you are a trader, you are likely to work with options or highly volatile stocks, or to trade futures directly. Traders accept higher levels of risk. A good balance between investing and trading is found in ETFs and indices, where it is possible to invest long-term, even in traditionally short-term products like futures contracts.

2. *Risk and opportunity are two sides of one coin.* The degree of risk is directly connected to the opportunity for profit. Many traders tend to focus on profit potential alone, often ignoring risk and simply hoping to beat the odds. It is true that when playing poker, you can occasionally bluff and win a pot with a terrible hand; in trading, this is much less likely. The key to successful trading is to create profits consistently, because beating the averages is impossible unless you employ a smart system. So low risk is married to low profit potential but a high level of safety; and if you go for high returns, you also need to accept higher than average risks.

3. *Risk comes in many forms.* It is easy to think of risk as a singular attribute of a company or product. But in fact, there are many different forms of risk. The best known of these is market risk, which is simply the risk that the market value of an investment will decline. But as this chapter demonstrates, risk is varied and multifaceted.

Knowledge risk is most often overlooked, especially in complex markets such as futures or options. You need to know the potential risks as well as potential profits, and also to appreciate the special trading rules and regulations, jargon, and technical tendencies of complex products. In addition, you cannot ignore diversification, interest, liquidity, leverage, and lost opportunity risk.

In the futures market, one type of risk that does not affect other markets as seriously is systematic risk, also called political risk. For example, if major conflicts in the Middle East curtail oil production or delivery, oil futures prices are likely to rise as a consequence. Political unrest in Asia may affect rice production and, as a result, futures prices; and similar systematic risks in many parts of the world can also affect coffee prices. This special kind of risk is more likely to affect futures contracts than many stocks, mutual funds, or real estate investments.

The Nature of Risk

All definitions of risk have to include the comparison of risk on two levels. First is that between risk and opportunity. The greater the opportunity, the greater the risk, and the smaller the opportunity, the smaller the risk. So if you are very conservative and you want to protect your capital—which is called the goal of "capital preservation"—then you have to be willing to accept smaller potential returns. Rather than chasing double-digit returns in some very volatile markets, you need to select very safe but low-yielding alternatives. For example, you can get an insured certificate of deposit yielding very low rates, but with virtual certainty that your money will be protected. The problem with low yields is that the combined effects of inflation and taxes may result in an after-tax lower value.

The second way to compare risks is to compare your personal risk tolerance with your financial objectives. Risk tolerance simply means the amount of risk that you can afford to take. If you cannot afford to lose any money from your portfolio, you should have your money in very safe investments. But if you can afford to take chances, then more volatile markets offering potentially greater rates of return could be appropriate for you. Your financial objectives also come into play, and that involves many considerations: income, available capital, age, knowledge of the markets, and number of years until your planned retirement.

Risk is widely misunderstood and mischaracterized in the markets. For example, you may hear that a particular investment is "risk-free." There is no such thing. In some market conditions, people have convinced themselves that it is impossible to lose money investing in real estate. This false premise contributed largely to the problems in many housing markets beginning in

2006. With excessive lending and poorly structured loan policies, many mistakes were made—zero-down loans, 125% equity loans, stated loans, and teaser rates in sub-prime packages. All of these contributed to the speculative abuses in real estate, proving that in fact, this market has a lot of risk.

Now consider the opposite end of the spectrum, the extremely "safe" investment. You can get a guaranteed rate of return in an insured account in a savings institution, but is that investment actually safe? If both inflation and taxes reduce your gross return to the point that you do not break even on an after-tax basis, you are losing.

To calculate your breakeven return, divide the current rate of inflation by your after-tax annual income. For the rate of inflation, you may use the Consumer Price Index (CPI), which you can find at the federal Bureau of Labor Statistics' Web site, www.bls.gov/cpi. Your after-tax rate of return is your income after deducting the effective tax rate for both federal and state income. This is the percentage of tax you are assessed based on your taxable income. For example, if your effective tax rate on your federal return is 28% and your state's rate is 8%, your combined tax rate is 36%. This means that your net after-tax income is 64%. So if you assume the current inflation rate is 3%, you would calculate breakeven as follows: divide 3% by the net after-tax income of 64%. You need to earn 4.7% just to break even. Figure 4-1 shows the formula for calculating the required breakeven rate.

Table 4-1 shows a summary of rates you must earn to break even—assuming various rates of inflation and combined federal and state tax rates.

For example, if you assume 4% inflation and your combined federal and state income tax rates are 38%, you need to get a 6.5% return just to break even. This would not be an exceptionally high tax rate, when you consider the levels of tax in many states. For example, current federal rates can be as high as 35%. State taxes can be high as well, with Utah the highest at 9.5%. Combined with the maximum federal rate of 35%, your combined rate could be 44.5% of taxable income. Other high tax states include California (9.3% maximum), Iowa (8.98%), and New Jersey (8.97%).

FIGURE 4.1. BREAKEVEN RETURN

breakeven return

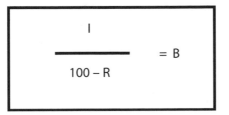

$$\frac{I}{100 - R} = B$$

where I = rate of inflation
R = effective federal and state tax rate
B = breakeven return.

TABLE 4.1. BREAKEVEN RATES

	INFLATION RATE					
Effective tax rate	1%	2%	3%	4%	5%	6%
14%	1.2%	2.3%	3.5%	4.7%	5.8%	7.0%
16%	1.2	2.4	3.6	4.8	6.0	7.1
18%	1.2	2.4	3.7	4.9	0.1	7.0
20%	1.3	2.5	3.8	5.0	6.3	7.5
22%	1.3	2.6	3.8	5.1	6.4	7.7
24%	1.3%	2.6%	3.9%	5.3%	6.6%	7.9%
26%	1.4	2.7	4.1	5.4	6.8	8.1
28%	1.4	2.8	4.2	5.6	6.9	8.3
30%	1.4	2.9	4.3	5.7	7.1	8.6
32%	1.5	2.9	4.4	5.9	7.4	8.8
34%	1.5%	3.0%	4.5%	6.1%	7.6%	9.1%
36%	1.6	3.1	4.7	6.3	7.8	9.4
38%	1.6	3.2	4.8	6.5	8.1	9.7
40%	1.7	3.3	5.0	6.7	8.3	10.0
42%	1.7	3.4	5.2	6.9	8.6	10.3
44%	1.8%	3.6%	5.4%	7.1%	8.9%	10.7%
46%	1.9	3.7	5.6	7.4	9.3	11.1
48%	1.9	3.8	5.8	7.7	9.6	11.5
50%	2.0	4.0	6.0	8.0	10.0	12.0
52%	2.1	4.2	6.3	8.3	10.4	12.5

Valuable Resource: The IRS Web site (www.irs.gov/formspubs/article/
0,,id = 150856,00.html) lists current federal tax rates. A listing of state
income tax rates is at www.taxadmin.org/fta/rate/ind_inc.html.

You may think of the combined effects as inflation/tax risk, something often invisible but all too real. You might think you're doing well with that 5% or 6% return on your investments, only to discover that you are losing purchasing power over time due to inflation and taxes. This reality also points out the flaw in seeking low-yielding, highly safe investments. That safety may come at a price, a net after inflation/tax loss.

So risk cannot be isolated from opportunity. This is the reality you face in all types of markets. The solution for most people is to figure out a way to create acceptable risk levels in their portfolios, in order to generate needed rates of return. For many, simply preserving the net purchasing power of their money is good enough; for others, investing is a way to earn more and even to get rich. The speculator hopes to beat the averages by exceeding the averages, and a lot of energy is put into trying to find the right system. Whether that even exists is debatable.

Your Personal Risk Profile

Before deciding whether any market is appropriate, you need to define your own risk profile. This involves analysis of risk levels as well as personal risk tolerance and investing objectives. A lot of energy is expended in this effort, often by financial planners and advisors trying to create programs for clients. Realistically, many planners are simply commission-based salespeople who use the financial planning process as a sales tool. In the final analysis, each person is responsible for developing these definitions. A qualified financial professional can be helpful by asking the right questions; but ultimately, you have to keep in mind several qualifications:

1. *Defining your risk profile is useful only if it leads to specific investing limits and alternatives.* You can and should work on your own personal risk profile. However, it is not enough to define yourself as "conservative" or "moderate" when it comes to your

investing requirements. You need to develop a list of investment alternatives that fit or do not fit your profile. For example, a very cautious person may want to avoid options or directly owned futures, focusing on blue-chip stocks yielding good dividends, or employing mutual funds and ETFs. Within the ETF or index fund world, it may be appropriate to focus on commodities or a specific market sector. The point is that you cannot know where to invest your money until you know how much opportunity/ risk is appropriate for you.

2. *The risk profile has to be followed and respected to be effective.* Many people describe themselves as "value investors" or "conservative" and then go out and speculate wildly with futures, options, or volatile stocks. When they lose money, they are puzzled. But the reason is clear. If a person does not adhere to a well-defined risk profile, there is no discipline within the portfolio, and no program of progressive investing can be expected. In a well-defined risk profile, profit or loss occurs at expected levels and at acceptable levels.

3. *Risk profiles change continually, so you need to review and update as your life changes.* The major events in your life affect and alter your risk profile. The most obvious change is improved knowledge and experience as an investor, because expanded information tends to broaden your potential markets, but this is only one aspect of a life change. More important are events like marriage, having a child, buying a home, divorce, poor health, a child's college education, beginning a new career, changes in income level, losing a job, starting a business, and poor health or death of a family member. Each of these changes creates an entirely new risk profile. That means that investment plans you had a few years ago probably do not work any longer, not only because your knowledge and experience have grown but also because your financial and personal circumstances have changed as well. These changes require adjustments to insurance (life, health, disability, auto, homeowners) as well as to the mix of investments you hold in your portfolio. A young single person can afford to speculate and even to take losses, but a head of household on a tight budget has to select investments

that are not going to lose. The overall portfolio, including a family home, savings, and retirement plans, and a portfolio involving stocks, bonds, and potentially futures, can be structured in many ways. For those who are most conservative, pooled investments like mutual funds, index funds, and ETFs are quite appealing. For the more experienced investor (or for conservative investors willing to diversify their portfolios into individual issues) some direct ownership is appropriate as well. It is not the same for everyone; designing a portfolio has to be based on (a) specific current risk profile, (b) personal risk tolerance, and (c) knowledge about each market under consideration.

4. *The risk profile and risk tolerance levels are not the whole story.* In addition to defining yourself in terms of experience, knowledge, capability, and personal preferences, you also need to assess markets and market conditions. All markets are in a never-ending state of change. This means that all products—stocks, futures contracts, real estate—are in a constant state of movement. So even after you have defined appropriate markets and products, you also need to study and track specific markets. So risk is never going to remain the same in every condition. You might hear it said that "the futures market is too risky," but this is not the same at all times. First of all, buying a futures ETF is not as risky as buying a specific futures contract, based on diversification. In addition, markets are changing constantly. At some times, agricultural futures are weak and energy futures are strong. These situations may evolve and reverse status over time. Stocks may also be strong or weak, and specific stock sectors change as well. In 2007, the energy sector was the strongest and financial and housing sectors were the weakest. In past years (and surely in future years), those weak sectors were market leaders. To set your portfolio properly, you need to define your personal risk profile and review it continuously, and also to evaluate current market conditions for the various markets that interest you. If one is weak today, just wait a few months. The cycles never stop moving.

■ Futures to Hedge Other Market Risks

The concept of "risk transference" takes on a lot of meaning when you analyze the futures market. The market was created to transfer risk between producers and buyers, providing some assurances and certainty on both sides. The buyer uses futures contracts to guarantee a market and a price for a commodity. Thus, if there are few buyers and an abundance of a crop, the futures contract transfers the producer's risk to the buyer. And the buyer also benefits. If there is a poor crop and scarce commodities one year, prices will soar. But owning a futures contract fixes the price so that the buyer also has certainty. Because the market price trend can go either way, both sides benefit from this basic form of risk transference.

The concept applies to other markets as well. Futures contracts are used to protect one position against another. For example, financial institutions are very sensitive to changes in interest rates, and if rates go up so does the cost of lending money. Likewise, if rates go down, existing mortgages and other loans will be replaced with lower-rate debt. So as interest rates (the price of money) are uncertain, financial institutions can use interest futures to protect their markets in the coming year.

Hedging between stocks and commodities is also common. For example, a speculator might be long on the energy sector while going short on energy futures, or vice versa. One position offsets the other, so that an unexpectedly large price swing will help avoid large losses. The majority of hedging activity of this type is going to occur in the futures market, meaning trading in the contract. In comparison, some use the cash market as a hedge. This refers to actual commodities apart from the futures market. Whereas the futures contract involves a contractual right, the cash market involves buying and selling of agricultural products, precious metals, livestock, or financial products.

So hedging in one respect refers to fixing future prices in the cash market. A jeweler wants to buy a quantity of gold, or a grower needs corn; so the contract is used to fix the price in the immediate future. For most investors not interested in getting 40,000 pounds of anything, hedging is going to occur strictly in the contract itself. Exchange members transact futures contract trades, as opposed to actual producers and users in the cash market. This futures exchange market is accessed through a series of clearinghouses, indices, or ETFs used by traders.

Hedging within the futures market enables individuals to apply significant leverage. You can control a large amount of a commodity for relatively low risks and, if you trade through a pooled investment, for relatively little risk. Hedging may be long (involving the purchase of contracts when you expect prices to rise) or short (when you sell futures contracts expecting prices to fall).

Successful hedging must involve an understanding of how markets interact and perform. For example, many stock-based fundamentals (earnings and revenue, dividend yield, P/E ratio, competitive factors) affect stock prices outside of any futures contracts or cash prices. At the same time, the underlying commodity is going to react to price competition and supply and demand. For example, energy futures contracts are going to rise or fall based on levels of the Strategic Petroleum Reserve, OPC policies and changes, and political sensitivities. When former Prime Minister of Pakistan Benazir Bhutto was assassinated at the end of December 2007, oil futures prices rose within two days from $93 to $97 per barrel before retreating somewhat. The point is, futures prices are going to be highly reactive to political events or so-called systematic risk. Figure 4-2 summarizes the two-day record of oil prices, reflected on December 27 and 28, 2007, in the February contract for light crude oil (CLG). (The futures contract for light crude oil is "CL," and the February contract is identified with "G.")

Notice how the price spiked on December 27 and 28. Prices then fell quickly back from $98 per barrel down to $96. This is typical of a short-term reaction to systematic news. The tendency is for prices to react very quickly and then to return to "normal" trading levels based on the previous trading range.

Even short-term price movement does not always work efficiently. Hedgers recognize the fact that futures and cash prices do not always change to the same degree. This opens up the potential for making hedge transactions. But this is only appropriate for speculators or for those who understand the nature of the futures market versus the cash market. A hedge of this type may easily be unbalanced, because you cannot divide a futures contract. So a trade in such a contract is for 100% of the minimum unit size. Thus, the cash position and futures position will not always be unified; you may need to underhedge or overhedge your positions.

It is also possible to hedge *between* commodities. For example, palm oil and soybean oil can be hedged against one another. In the

FIGURE 4.2. LIGHT CRUDE OIL FEBRUARY CONTRACT, DECEMBER 27 AND 28, 2007

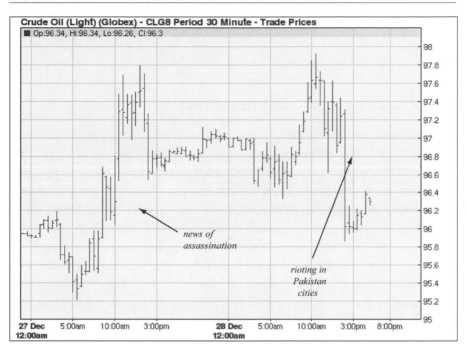

Source: Charts provided courtesy of TradingCharts.com: http//futures.tradingcharts.com; created with SuperCharts by Omega Research © 1997.

emerging market for ethanol, it is also likely that ethanol futures could be hedged against light sweet crude or even against corn prices. If you appreciate the interaction between two different commodities, many hedging opportunities can be identified. However, you also need to ensure that you know the risks involved in offsetting long and short positions.

A ratio hedge is another version. When the cash and futures price are relatively far apart, loading up one side of the hedge can make sense, anticipating that the gap is going to close as delivery date approaches. You can use futures in many of the same ways that stock traders use options, and the ratio hedge can be very similar to the stock-based options ratio write. In that transaction, a ratio may be higher or lower than the number of 100-lot shares. For example, if you own 400 shares and write five calls against the position, it creates a ratio write. It can be viewed as four covered calls and one naked, or as a 5-to-4 ratio write. In futures contracts, a similar hedging occurs between cash and futures prices, and the risks are similar. But the relationship between cash and futures prices may be more difficult to understand than the relationship between stock price and option premium levels.

Knowledge and Familiarity Risk

As the previous section demonstrates, the level of knowledge about a market and its strategies determine appropriate and inappropriate strategies. If you do not understand how futures hedging works, you are not alone. It makes no sense, though, to expect yourself to place capital at risk without thoroughly understanding the mechanics of the trade and the level of risk involved.

The two-part risk of *knowledge* and *familiarity* work together to target specific markets and strategies that can work for you. For example, you might be very familiar with real estate because you own a house. Thus, you know all about mortgage amortization, fire insurance, and maintenance. This does not mean you will also be familiar with the investment aspects or risks of becoming a landlord. The intricacies of working with tenants, qualifying for mortgages for nonoccupied homes, and managing investment property cash flow are entirely apart from your knowledge as a homeowner. Taking this comparison to another level, even if you are knowledgeable about and familiar with residential investment property, that does not mean you also understand the market for commercial, industrial, or lodging investments. These markets all contain separate and distinct levels of risk, because the attributes of a "good" versus "bad" investment are going to be based on market trends completely different than those for residential properties.

In the stock market, you are probably very well versed in mutual funds and many different market sectors. But familiarity with retail, energy, and financial sectors does not mean you also have familiarity or knowledge concerning biotech or defense sectors. In fact, it is reasonable to point out that not all stocks are the same since each sector contains its own unique and different risks. Many people assume that knowledge about fundamental and technical analysis is enough to pick stocks. Merely applying a few criteria indicate strength and weakness, safety and risk, and profit or loss. However, given the market cycles for each sector, this is not always true.

You need both knowledge and familiarity on many levels to avoid the risk of making mistakes. The levels include broad markets with their special trading rules, jargon, and limitations; market sectors and their economic cycles; and individual companies, issuers, or commodities with their own market positions and interactions. For example, a market leader such as ExxonMobil, McDonald's, or Microsoft defines one attribute. You may want to invest in the company that dominates its industry. In futures contracts, the same rules apply. Just as McDonald's stock interacts with Burger King, numerous interactions occur between and among commodities. Consider the interaction between corn and ethanol, or between interest rate futures and currency exchange rate futures. These are directly related due to economic cause and effect in the markets. You should never study or evaluate one futures contract, or stock or bond, or other investment product in isolation.

The trends in energy prices affect McDonald's stock value, because the company relies on delivery, meaning trucks, which in turn has everything to do with fuel costs. So rising energy prices ultimately also mean higher prices at the golden arches, or lower sales volume, or both. For the astute trader observing the interaction of these different markets, some opportunities become apparent. However, before you are prepared to take advantage of the economic and cyclical trends, you need to be completely knowledgeable about how those markets work; and familiar with the risks and potential rewards they entail.

Market Risk

The best-known and understood of all risks is market risk. Simply put, this is the risk that price will move in an opposite direction than what you desire. Many people who buy any investment product make the basic error of assuming that their entry price represents a "zero point" in the price trend. So you buy stock at $40 per share expecting it to rise, but forgetting that it can also fall. In this example, an investor has ignored market risk.

A short seller takes the opposite version of a "zero point" strategy. Because a sell order is an opening phase, the short seller expects price to fall. If this is not the case, price will rise and the short position loses out. This is true in stocks as well as in futures contracts. If you track the futures price trend, you see that most of the action occurs in the contract one out from the next delivery date. Price estimates of futures traders are continually in flux, and the further out, the more uncertainty in price levels. If you take a short position in a futures contract, you can always roll forward to a later delivery date. But what happens if the price of the underlying commodity just continues to rise? At some point, you can no longer sustain your short position. So in this instance, ignoring the market risk could cause a considerable net loss in the position, not to mention tying up margin account levels for the indefinite future. Even if you short through indices or ETFs, you should not ignore market risk because it exists for every long and short position.

Until you understand how markets move to the point where risks can be fully appreciated, short positions (whether through direct or pooled venues) can be quite risky. Just as a novice stock investor is discouraged from shorting stock due to risk levels involved, a newcomer to the futures market needs to spend time becoming familiar with the markets as a first step.

Market risk applies to all markets and even to fully diversified portfolios. In stocks as well as in commodities, general economic trends tend to affect entire markets. So commodity prices are likely to "tend to trend" in the same direction. As prices rise due to inflation or a weakened U.S. dollar, commodity prices are likely to move generally in the same direction. You cannot study or analyze any commodity in isolation from the overall market or from the broader, longer-term economic trend.

Stock market investors have known this for a long time. A historically consistent growth in prices have pampered real estate investors, so when prices stop growing or fall, there is a tendency to think the entire economy will come crashing down. But 2007 demonstrated that even when a major sector like the financial sector is soft, even when housing is weak and banks and brokerages are losing price value, the overall economy can remain strong and in an upward trend. In the futures market, the interaction between commodities and stocks is obvious and can be witnessed by comparing sector ETFs or index funds with commodity prices. But on a more permanent level, futures trends increasingly reflect trends in the global market as well. In the past, distinctions were made between domestic and import markets. Today, while balance of trade continues to be used as one of many economic indicators, the economy has become truly global and futures prices are no longer distinguished by country or by region. Thus, market risk has also become global in nature, a reality that affects how futures trading takes place today and in the future.

Systematic and Lost Opportunity Risks

World events are very troubling to futures traders in the United States because they are beyond the control of the individual and even of the markets. Even the U.S. government, with its political power, has little to say about OPEC-based decisions regarding production, refinery levels, or oil prices. While domestic agriculture is very productive, the United States imports some agricultural products and exports others. And many basic materials are imported as well, such as coffee, for example.

Global systematic risk, mostly beyond the control of an exchange, an individual company, or any one government, definitely affects futures price levels. World political events, especially disasters or volatility in another country, have immediate impact on futures prices.

This reality is both a negative and a potentially positive reality. It is negative because such political events are beyond our control and many commodities come from areas that are very unstable. The Middle East, where a large portion of oil is generated, has been unstable for many decades without signs of improvement. In fact, conditions there have only worsened in recent years. But this can be positive as well. Prices reflect instability and the potential for drastic price changes. Recognizing this, even the most systematically sensitive commodity is likely to trade with great volatility. For the futures speculator willing to take on the risks, this realization points the way to profit potential. The *risk* of political uncertainty represents an equally volatile *opportunity*. This means that uncertainty may discount the futures contract in a specific area due to this unknown systematic risk, but at the same time it presents an opportunity for great profits due to the same influences.

Closely related to systematic risk is another variety, known as lost opportunity risk. In terms of the futures market, this refers to the backward-looking realization that some event or series of events led up to price movement. If only you had been hedged into a position in a commodity, you would have made a profit if and when the events unfolded.

Lost opportunity also refers to the problem of having capital completely committed to a series of positions, meaning it is impossible to take action when new opportunities present themselves. This has relevance in the futures market in respect to margin limits, so a trader who is fully leveraged cannot jump when presented with a newly emerging trend.

Another version of lost opportunity arises when a portfolio is overdiversified or overallocated. For example, if you take a large portion of your capital and use it for a down payment on an investment property, you have a series of advantages: cash flow from an income stream, tax benefits, and traditionally growing market values. But what if the market slows, stops, or falls? In that case, your capital is tied up in an asset that is not growing. Meanwhile, other investments and other markets might be moving very rapidly forward, but because you committed your capital to an illiquid asset like real estate, you cannot take action. This is also a lost opportunity.

Even futures traders who hedge positions can overextend their margin leverage, creating a different version of lost opportunity. If such a trader realizes—too late—that the hedge position involving offsetting long and short positions led to missed chances to do more in other markets or in different configurations of futures contracts, then the strategy could prove to be misguided.

Lost opportunity risk is expensive even when a specific strategy is successful. If you recognize that other choices would have been more profitable or better leveraged, the existing position suffers from lost opportunity risk. Traders need to be aware of leveraging limitations and margin requirements before tying up capital for too long a period. In the fast-moving futures market, lost opportunity can translate to lost profits as well as to future uncertainty; if you do not want to fall into the same trap in future trades, it is all too easy to hesitate and pass on otherwise sound strategic choices.

Speculation Risk

The common problems traders encounter in overusing margin accounts or forgetting to respect their own self-defined risk profile are well known. But many investors forget to also make a distinction between *investing* and *speculating*.

Risk and opportunity are clearly associated and, in fact, attributes of the same reality. They are simply two sides of product volatility. Market risk is the risk that an investment's value will decline, and, in comparison, speculation risk is the risk that highly volatile investments will wipe out a large portion of your capital. Speculators are invariably short-term traders. In comparison, investors usually think in longer time frames, and select investments with months or years in mind. So in studying the fundamental strength or weakness of a company, stock takes on relative value in the mind of the investor. The speculator is concerned only with how price is likely to change in the immediate future—days or even hours.

When the speculative approach is applied to futures trading, it is easy to see why this fast-moving market is so appealing. Many would-be futures traders stay out of this market for several reasons, but would gladly partake if these inhibiting factors could be overcome. Among the reasons that stock speculators do not always trade in futures, are:

1. *The market is not as easy to enter and exit.* The stock investor can open an online brokerage account for no cost and fund the account with a few hundred dollars. It is easy and cheap to buy and sell shares online for very low costs, often as low as $7 per trade. The futures market is not as widely available. To buy and sell futures contracts directly, you need to work through a clearinghouse or commodities broker, and all trades have to go through an exchange member. When you compare the futures market to the stock market, you immediately realize that rules for the futures ex-

changes are many years behind the liberated access that stock investors enjoy.

2. *Stocks are widely well understood, but futures are more complex.* Most people with money to invest understand how stocks work, and also what factors influence value. The market supply and demand movement is easily anticipated, and events like earnings reports, mergers, and changes in credit rating are seen immediately in the effect on stock prices. The futures market is more complex, with the factors influencing price often based on worldwide economic and political factors, or on price trends not as apparent to most observers. Market tracking for stocks is a form of instant gratification, but in the futures market, short-term volatility occurs but it is more likely that change is going to be based on subtle, longer-term trends.

3. *Factors affecting value are not the same as stock market factors.* The stock investor can analyze the reasons for price strength or weakness and, with indicators like the P/E ratio, can also develop a comparative analysis of how the market perceives a company and its stock as a long-term investment. Current price volatility further quantifies risk. But in the futures market, there are many indirect influences affecting price and interactions that are difficult to gauge. For example, the emerging demand for ethanol has not only created a new commodity. It has also affected agricultural prices as corn has become more than a source of food and feed. It will also affect the range of energy futures based on market anticipation of ethanol as a replacement fuel in coming years. Whether any of this has a long-term effect or not remains to be seen; but today, the potential ramifications of this new energy resource has complicated many related futures prices as well.

4. *Stocks can be held long-term, but futures contracts rarely exist for more than a few months.* The stock investor can act as both long-term investor and short-term speculator. This choice provides one of many forms of potential diversification. But in the futures market, there is no long-term investment. Traders are involved with a contract that has a delivery date coming up quite soon, usually within a year or less. The only way to maintain a position in the market beyond that is to roll contracts forward to avoid delivery

dates, which is exactly what pooled investors do. You can also buy shares in pooled investments like futures ETFs, so that your shares of the fund are permanent. But even with this approach, the actual holdings in the fund are rolled continuously.

Speculators—including anyone who buys or sells futures contracts through a clearinghouse or commodities broker—are short-term strategists. But they operate in the same way that stock market speculators do. In fact, chart patterns for futures trading are analyzed in very much the same way as they are for stocks. It is important to remember the major distinction between investing and speculating. When you act as an investor, you are usually willing to wait out a price trend, and you are likely to select investments based on fundamental trends and indicators. When you act as a speculator, it is more likely that you will focus on price as a primary selection criterion, and track price trends through chart analysis. Speculation is short-term, meaning positions are going to be kept open for only a few days. Some speculators like to move in and out of open positions over a period of hours only; so the range of speculation based on time can involve a very short time horizon.

Diversification and Allocation Risks

Just as the distinction between investing and speculating is often fuzzy, the concept of *diversification* is widely misunderstood. It is often characterized as a sidebar to a portfolio system, or as some type of automatic process apart from other considerations. However, if used properly, diversification actually serves as a risk management tool. This is where futures trading as a hedge and as a form of diversification becomes so valuable.

There are many forms of diversification, the relatively simple ones focus on a portfolio involving stocks only:

- Owning stock of more than one company
- Diversifying by sectors with dissimilar economic cycles
- Employing equity mutual funds

These three levels of diversification are certainly effective for spreading risks among stocks and within the stock market. Going beyond this, however, diversification may also involve hedging, and two specific markets are obvious choices: options and futures. In the options market, options can be used to insure paper profits (long puts), take advantage of short-term price declines (long calls), or to create additional income (covered calls). In the futures market, contracts can be used to offset and hedge positions in specific sectors. For example, a long position in energy sector stocks can be hedged with a short position in energy futures contracts. There are also ETFs on the market designed specifically to short stock or futures markets.

Beyond diversification, the process of *allocation* involves investment in separate markets. The usual ones involved are stocks, debt instruments (bonds or money market), and real estate. In many applications, the "appropriate" level of allocation is determined on a broad and arbitrary percentage basis. You may read online or in the financial press that "you should be allocated 40% stocks, 25% real estate, and 35% debt." However, when advice is given broadly to the entire market, the underlying philosophy is that allocation has to be based on market conditions and applies to all investors. A conflicting opinion states an approach completely different: Each investor should allocate the items in his or her portfolio based on perceptions of markets, risk profile, and risk tolerance. This is a more difficult interpretation of asset allocation, but also a more logical one.

There also is a natural conflict between investing and speculating, so thinking about futures as an aspect of a permanent portfolio is contrary to the nature of the instrument. However, if you trade through a futures ETF or index, it is conceivably possible to keep shares indefinitely and to treat a futures package as an investment. Another approach is to divide a total portfolio between investment assets and speculative assets. You may apply a relatively small portion of the total to speculative moves, such as buying of options or futures contracts; trading in volatile stocks; or buying hard assets (gold, for example) in the belief that prices are going to rise.

Diversification is certainly a method for managing risk, by spreading it around to avoid a 100% decline in a portfolio. However, two specific kinds of diversification-related risk are possible. The best known is underdiversification, in which your portfolio is not effectively diversified at all. For example, owning shares in four different energy companies, financials, or retail concerns is *not* diversification. Because sectors tend to rise and fall as a group, it is not true diversification to own many of the same kinds of companies.

A second and often overlooked risk is overdiversification. Many of the larger equity mutual funds have so many billions of dollars in their portfolio (along with restrictions limiting how much they are allowed to own in any one company) that they virtually duplicate the broader market. As a consequence, any breakout returns are unlikely. In fact, only about 10% of all mutual funds beat the S&P 500, indicating that mutual fund investing is one form of overdiversification. The solution is to find relatively small funds that do beat the market.

With ETFs, a similar problem is seen even by individual sectors. Why buy an entire sector when you could focus on one or two companies that lead and outperform its competitors? ETFs also tend to perform at the mediocre average of their portfolio. An exception to this is found in funds focusing on futures investments. Because investing in futures otherwise requires going through a commodities broker (which can be very expensive), picking one of the growing number of futures ETFs makes sense. It is cheaper than buying directly, and of course far less risky than direct ownership.

You can also overdiversify within a portfolio of directly owned stocks. For example, you can effectively diversify risk with four or five stocks in different market sectors and subject to different economic cycles. So it may be effective to own varying numbers of shares in only four companies. However, if you were to own half as many shares spread over eight different companies, is that effective? The risk is that this will overdiversify your portfolio, resulting in no more profits and potentially lower profits overall.

One solution to overdiversification is to focus on hedging rather than spreading risks. For many seasoned investors, this idea is revolutionary, but it should not be. In other words, you do not need to buy more different company stocks to reduce risks and, in fact, that may only *add* to the portfolio's market risk. As an alternative, you can focus on a very small number of diverse stock holdings, and then hedge using futures contracts. The inherent risk of futures is separately diversified by limiting exposure to indices or ETFs designed to spread capital among commodities. In Chapter 2, several futures-specific indices were examined, as well as ETFs with highly focused commodity sectors or ranges of diversified futures holdings.

So a possible solution to the problems of overdiversification involves three possible ideas:

1. *Focusing the equity portion of your portfolio in a small number of stocks.* Rather than trying to accomplish complete risk reduction in a stocks-only portfolio, pick four excellent companies (for example, low P/E, competitive dividend yield, consistent growth in revenue and earnings, and low debt ratio). Focus the core of your portfolio on holdings equally distributed among these companies. Strive for an equal-dollar investment in each of the companies, remembering that odd lot purchases are not much more expensive today than round lots. You do not have to buy 100 shares.

2. *Hedging the portfolio of stocks with futures indices or ETFs.* As a replacement for the perceived need to reduce risk with broad diversification, look for ways to hedge your long equity position. Because markets tend to trend as groups, spreading your portfolio among many different stocks is not necessarily effective, so hedging is going to be a better strategy to protect yourself. Consider both the futures and options markets as potential hedging instruments.

3. *Accomplishing further asset allocation involving debt or real estate, based on your individual risk profile.* Many investors are not content to diversify their portfolios or even to hedge positions; they want to accomplish a long-term allocation of investments. If you are buying your family home, you already have a considerable position in real estate; and although you should not think of your home solely as an investment, it does have many valuable investment attributes. These include the long-term tendency to increase in value and to hedge against inflation (for example, a fixed-rate mortgage remains unchanged even when other costs rise). You also enjoy considerable tax benefits via home ownership and even when you

sell. (Not only are you allowed to deduct interest and property taxes, but upon sale of a home you have lived in for at least two of the past five years, you escape all federal taxes on up to $500,000 in profit for a married couple, or $250,000 for single people.) So you may already be allocated effectively in real estate.

Buying shares of income mutual funds also diversifies your equity positions by adding bonds. You can also use ETFs or relatively new Exchange-Traded Notes (ETNs) to allocate to the debt markets.

Futures indices and ETFs accomplish two kinds of allocation. First, they place a portion of your capital in a position that hedges your equity holdings. Second, they take a short-term *trading* market and transfer it to an *investing* market. Because shares of index or ETF-based futures will appreciate as futures markets perform well relative to equities, your shares in these pooled accounts will act the same as they do in mutual fund accounts. So even when your index or ETF is involved with short-term futures contracts and rolling them forward endlessly, your shares act just like other investments. If you choose well and the market performs as you expect, your share value is going to rise.

The potential for success in the futures market relies on determining how to reduce risk, and that requires an understanding of how risk works. When you realize that hedging is more effective than simply owning a greater number of different stocks, the value of pooled futures investing is exciting. In the next section of four chapters, you will see how to reach the market, analyze its strength or weakness, and identify the overall economic mood. Because commodities reflect economic conditions directly, it is crucial to identify whether the economy is growing or receding. This process begins by defining specifically how orders get placed, which is the topic of Chapter 5.

PART 2

REACHING THE MARKET

5 Yr. Treasury Not
June   111-087 111
Sept   115-185 110-

2 Yr. Treasury Note
June   106-007 106-

30 Day Federal Fund
April   97.735 97.7
May   97.940 97.94

1 Month Libor (CME)-
May   97.2100 97.230
June   97.2850 97.2950

Eurodollar (CME)-$1,000.0
May   97.1450 97.1925
June   97.1200 97.2150
Sept   97.0400 97.1500
Dec   96.8600 96.9700

Currency Futures

C H A P T E R   5

ORDER PLACEMENT

W hen you begin trading in any market, one of the first questions has to be, How do I place an order? For many novices, this is a great concern. You may know enough to realize that if you make a mistake it can cost you thousands of dollars. In this chapter, you will find discussion of many order specifications, limits, how orders track, margin rules, and more.

It is equally important to know what to buy or sell, of course. You should base this decision on a range of fundamental and technical tests, and the chapters that follow cover this. As a first step, however, this chapter covers the mechanics of order placement in detail. If you end up buying a futures index or ETF, your task is easy. Because these convenient pools trade just like stocks, they can be traded easily and directly through your brokerage account.

For example, if you have an online stock trading account, you can enter the symbol GSG and find information on the GSCI Commodity Indexed Trust (see Chapter 2). You can buy or sell shares in this index as easily and as quickly as you can trade shares of stock. Options are also available on this index. As of January 2, 2008, the fund's value was approximately $54 per share. The April 2008 $55 option could be bought for about $225. You could also get a quote on the StreetTRACKS Gold Shares ETF (GLD), which provides the same range of information and ease of trading. There are no options on this ETF, but many others do offer them.

If you decide to buy or sell futures contracts directly, you will be working through a commodity broker, pool, or manager. Most people will find that using indices and ETFs makes more sense in terms of cost, diversification, and risk. However, if you do want to go the direct route, then you need to know all about how order processing works. Unlike the buying and selling of index or ETF shares, direct trading is more complex.

Order Specifications

Whenever you enter orders (in any market), there are a number of order specifications you need to know. These seem quite basic, but if you make a mistake it can be a costly one. For example, if you enter a "sell" instead of a "buy" or put in the symbol for live cattle (LC) instead of cocoa (CC), the mistake could be a costly one. So order specifications are very precise and critical, and should be double-checked.

The specifications are not unique to futures trading. They apply—at times with different names—to stocks, mutual funds, ETFs, indices, options, and other markets—and they boil down to a series of terms and conditions. Most people will prefer to have their set of criteria met before allowing an order to go forward. A simplified method is to place an order for immediate execution based on price movement in a specific futures contract; others will place standing orders to be executed only if specific conditions are met. Once you place orders, you can limit potential losses by placing limits or stops. In that situation, a transaction is set to occur as soon as a price level is met or passed. These conditions apply to all markets, and not just to futures.

The specifications for futures contracts are:

> *Action*—simply the distinction between an order to *buy* and an order to *sell*. If you accidentally enter a sell order, you will enter a short position and expose yourself to risks you did not intend. The importance of specifying buy or sell cannot

be emphasized too greatly. The risk levels are considerably greater for short positions in all markets, and futures are no exception. The chance for making mistakes are actually greater if you trade online, because there is no additional step where someone on the phone or across a desk can ask, "Are you sure?" So while online trading is fast, convenient, and cheap, it also requires greater diligence in ensuring that the terms—such as *buy* or *sell*—are carefully checked and then checked again before you hit that enter button.

Contract number—in other words, the number of contracts you intend to buy or sell. If you want to buy 10 but accidentally enter an order for 100, the error can be quite costly, for example, not to mention the difference in risk levels.

Specific commodity and delivery—the distinction between the dozens of possible futures contracts, and delivery defines the timing of and selection of a specific contract. Every commodity involves a delivery date, and the price varies between them. Some trade quarterly, others in consecutive months. However, if you study the quotations for any commodity, you immediately see that prices vary depending on the delivery month. The delivery month is summarized with a single digit added behind the one-or two-digit code distinguishing one product from the other.

You have to enter an order with careful selection of the one- or two-digit code for each product. For example, if you want to buy contracts of live cattle (LC) with an April delivery, you need to add a "J" to the live cattle designation and enter the order as LCJ. If you transpose one letter or simply enter the wrong month, you will trade in the wrong contract.

Exchange—the place where you want the order to be executed. Increasingly, as futures exchanges become more electronically operated and more competitive with each other, futures contracts are being offered on more than one exchange. The exchanges are the New York Mercantile Exchange (NYMEX), New York Board of Trade (NYBOT), Chicago Board of Trade (CBOT), Chicago Mercantile Exchange (CME), and the Intercontinental Exchange (ICE). Regional exchanges include two significant ones, the Minneapolis Grain Exchange (MGE) and the Kansas City Board of Trade (KCBT). Activity of the exchanges is regulated by the Commodity Futures Trading Commission (CFTC), the federal regulatory agency, and the National Futures Association (NFA), the industry's self-regulatory body.

Order type—which affects not only the price you pay or receive, but the timing and level of execution (the next section explains this in more detail).

Duration of order—meaning timing of execution. Some orders are put in for the current day only, whereas others—*open orders*—are set for execution without a time limit. If a day order cannot be filled today, it expires, so the distinction between order types by duration is a key attribute.

Price—which may be the most important attribute of all. Some trades are executed as market orders, meaning they are traded at whatever price prevails when execution occurs. Otherwise, a price or price threshold is specified and the order will only be filled if and when that level is reached or passed (below a specified level for buy orders or above a specified level for a sell order).

Types of Orders

You can place many different orders, each with its own special attributes. Some orders are qualified by timing (for example, day only or until canceled), and others are contingent (for example, limits or stops). Order types include:

Market—the easiest and most basic kind of order specifies that you are willing to have the order filled at the current market price or, if delayed, at any price available at the time of execution.

Market if touched—an order in which you specify a price; but the order is to be filled only if and when the price moves to that point (a buy market if touched order is normally placed below current price, and a sell market if touched is placed above). Once the price touches the specified level, the order is executed at current market price. That price may be higher or lower than the price specified in the order; the level acts as a trigger and not as an execution price.

Market on close—an order to buy or sell at the time the market closes for the day, at the closing price. This order specifies the time of execution rather than a specific price level.

Fill or kill—an order for immediate execution. If a matching order (a sell for your buy or a buy for your sell) cannot be found after three attempts, the order expires.

Good till canceled (GTC)—a specification that you want your order to stand until you cancel it. This is important in some situations because, without a GTC included, orders are assumed to be good only for the current session. As a result, all orders are treated as day orders (good for today only) unless they are placed as GTC.

One cancels other—a qualification when two orders are linked. The desire here is that whichever one gets executed first, the second is automatically canceled.

Limit—an order that is to be filled only at a specified price (or better). If you are buying, "better" means a lower price; and if you are selling, "better" means higher.

Stop—a condition in which the order gets executed if and when the market price is reached or moves through a specified level. But unlike the "market if touched" order, stops work in reverse. A buy stop occurs above market, and a sell stop occurs below.

Stop limit—a combination of a stop and a limit order. When the stop price is reached, the order converts to a limit order. So the transaction gets executed only if the market price has reached or surpassed the specified price.

Stop close only—an order that is to be executed when trading closes for the session, and only if and when the closing price is at or through the stop price you name.

Order types have developed based on what the market needs. Traders identify specific strategies for speculation and hedging activity, and as a result the order specifications and combinations become part of the trading system.

Order Tracking

Once an order has been placed, it moves through a series of steps before it has been finalized. Compared to the stock market, where you can execute your own orders online and fairly quickly with a minimum number of steps, the futures market is in many ways archaic. Change takes time. In fact, the advent of built-in diversification and ease of trading through futures indices and ETFs has left behind many of the traditional and slower methods. For most people, pooling is a great advantage. And it can be accomplished through an online broker, just as easily as trading in stock.

For those who remain interested in buying and selling directly, using a commodity clearinghouse or broker, an exchange member has to make every trade. This process may look simple; you simply place the order and await your confirmation by e-mail or through your online account. But a lot takes place in between, and the order process includes steps made by the following people:

Exchange clerks manage the order receipt at the exchange. Commodity brokers call orders in and clerks take them down by telephone, e-mail, or online account. The clerk passes the order to the floor broker.

Floor brokers are those manic people you see on television's financial shows, yelling back and forth and making hand signals while bidding prices with one another in the trading ring. A ring is used for trading in each type of futures contract. The floor broker has to find a matching price, locating a buyer for each sale order and a seller for each buy order. This occurs during the open outcry session each trading day. Once this match is made, the selling floor broker writes down the time on the order ticket, and then sends the competed order to the card clocker.

The floor trader also generates transactions. Also called the "local," the trader is the only person in the transaction actually allowed to trade in his or her personal account. In comparison, the floor broker's activity is limited to buy and sell for clients. Like the floor broker, the selling floor trader forwards completed orders to the card clocker.

Card clockers are those sitting in the center of the large trading ring on the floor of the exchange. He or she stamps every order placed, recording the price and time. Time-stamped tickets are then handed off to floor runners.

Floor runners gather completed, time-stamped order tickets and deliver them to data entry employees.

Data entry employees enter orders into the exchange system, and the price reporter notes the results in a handheld computer.

The price reporter conveys the latest price information from the automated system to the news ticker, which is viewed by traders and brokers.

Much of the activity in futures contract trading is done manually, and as many as 1,000 transactions per minute are recorded in this manner. In comparison, stock market transactions are mostly executed automatically. There remain some exchanges and markets that continue to rely on hand signals and bidding, but the vast majority of stock market trades are automated. The futures market continues to use these multiple stages with the traditional manual system, even though automated processing would be more efficient. Like all markets, it is only a matter of time before volume and demand mandate improvements.

In the history of the stock market, automation has enabled indices to rise to spectacular levels, and daily volume is today at levels unimaginable 20 or 30 years ago—mainly because stock trading used to rely on handwritten orders, stockbrokers, and telephone order placement. The systems in today's futures market are very much like stock trading two decades ago. Even orders placed online or by e-mail end up being transferred to handwritten orders, date-stamped and physically delivered from card clocker to floor runners, then to data entry. In other words, an automated order is copied out by hand, manually transferred, and then input into the exchange system.

It may take a few years for this system to be updated for modern technology. But just as Internet-based discount brokerage vastly changed the stock market, the same types of changes (as well as the growing popularly of futures indices and ETFs) will eventually bring the futures exchange systems into the twenty-first century.

Figure 5-1 summarizes the current exchange order processing system.

Margin Levels

The margin level is the level of cash or securities you are required to have in your account to cover trading activities. The account itself is a facility enabling traders to borrow cash to cover leveraged trades, and the rules are similar whether it is a stock or futures account.

Futures exchanges set margin policies, including the minimum amount required to be placed on deposit to enter an order. A second step in margin activity is the futures clearinghouse, which is required to adhere to exchange margin rules. Finally, the futures commission merchant—who has direct contact with traders placing orders—also has to adhere to the margin requirements. The FCM may also require higher margins from its trading clients.

So when an individual wants to trade through a direct account, he or she gives required margin funds to the FCM. This deposit is supposed to be deposited and held in separate accounts for each customer. The FCM pays margins to the clearinghouse, although its long and short positions may be largely offset, and only the net difference is actually transferred. The clearinghouse then sends net funds to the exchange or notifies the exchange that those margin deposits are on hand.

The exchange sets the rules. So minimum margin requirements can be revised at any time, and can also be used to keep volatility under control. The minimum levels can also be increased specifically for contracts in their spot months, when actual delivery of the underlying commodity could occur. When margin levels are changed, they are usually retroactive, so a margin call—demand

FIGURE 5.1. FUTURES TRADING SYSTEM

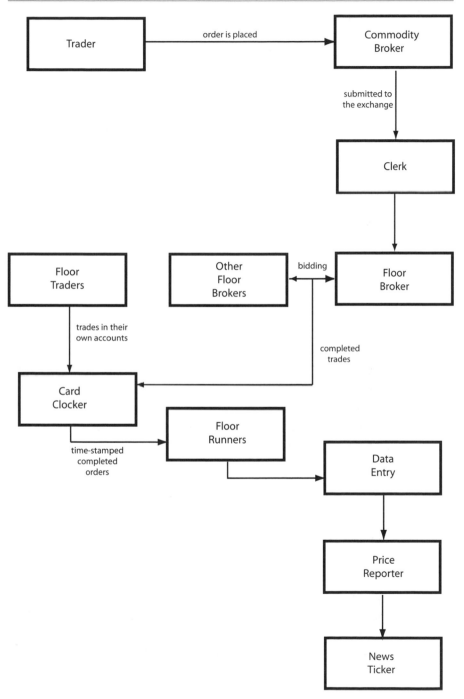

for additional funds to be deposited into the account—could occur whenever margin requirements are increased. If the margin requirement is lowered, that frees up equity and enables traders to remove funds or to increase the level of their open trades. Margin levels range between 5% and 15% of the delivery value of the contract, and these levels also vary by the specific commodity, based on minimum contract unit.

All exchanges—stock and futures—have systems in place to curtail excess volatility when markets move many points. The trading curbs used by stock exchanges are a well-known example. Futures exchanges employ a similar procedure called variation margin rules. When clearinghouse members have debit balances at the end of the trading day, their accounts are marked to the market. If variation margin rules are in effect, they are required to cover these debit balances before the opening of the next trading session. This ensures that the exchange will not end up with large debit balances on clearinghouse accounts. In other words, in times of great volatility, these steps ensure that cash on hand adequately covers open positions. While clearinghouses are usually allowed to float debit balances from day to day, margin calls do not occur when markets are orderly.

In addition to variation margin rules, exchanges limit the degree of movement allowed in any one futures contract during a single trading day. This prevents wild speculation and day trading in futures to excessive levels. The limit varies based on the prior day's settlement and applies in both up and down movements.

In addition to order placement, you need to know how to analyze the fundamental and technical aspects of futures. Simply knowing whether a market is strong or weak requires in-depth understanding of economic forces, interest in a particular commodity, the effect geopolitical events have on price levels, and factors that come into play. The next chapter introduces the various methods of fundamental analysis of futures, followed by a chapter concerning the technical side.

5 Yr. Treasury Not
June   111-087 111
Sept   113-185 110
2 Yr. Treasury Note
June   106-057 106-4
30 Day Federal Fund.
April   97.735 97.7
May   97.940 97.96
1 Month Libor (CME)-3
May   97.2100 97.230(
June   97.2850 97.2950
Eurodollar (CME)-31,000.0
May   97.1450 97.1925
June   97.1200 97.2150
Sept   97.0400 97.1500
Dec   96.8600 96.9700

Currency Futures

FUNDAMENTAL ANALYSIS
OF FUTURES

n the stock market, "fundamental analysis" refers to the financial position and history of a company. So the financial statements define strength or weakness, and the trend in revenue and net earnings demonstrates whether a company's situation is getting stronger or weaker. Long-term trends dominate fundamental analysis, where tests of capital strength, profitability, and closely related trends (price/earnings, dividend yield, competitive position, quality of management) also come into play.

In the futures market, the analysis has to be done quite differently. There is no company to analyze, but a range of products. These include energy, grains and oilseeds, livestock, lumber, precious metals, imports or tropical products, and financial futures. Each futures contract has a limited life, and today's range of delivery months will be replaced as later ones come on the scene and as current contracts expire. Because of this, futures are always a passing matter. However, the entire range of products should be quantified properly in terms of strength or weakness and price trends, using a fundamental approach. Because there is no specific corporate structure, fundamental analysis in the futures market has to be developed using national and international economics and economic trends.

Supply and Demand: An Economic Basic

Although the economic principle of "supply and demand" is widely discussed and known (especially among investors and traders), its attributes are mysterious. For example, the truth is that many traders fall into the trap of believing that their entry price—whether in stock, futures, or any other product—is the *starting point*, and that from there forward, value is going to build. In other words, traders often understand the theory of supply and demand, but they do not act as though it applies. When traders assume that their entry price is "zero" in terms of pending change, they are acting as though markets operate in a linear fashion, moving in a single line based primarily on the timing of their own decisions. This is irrational, but quite common.

Supply and demand define how and why prices change. In any investment or trading market, growing demand drives prices higher, and growing supply drives them lower. It makes sense. Price is going to change based on the scarcity (or lack of scarcity) of the product. Demand increases as prices fall, making it act opposite of the supply influence. Supply and demand are constantly in a battle for dominance.

There is really nothing mysterious about supply and demand at all, and prices change for good reasons. However, if you focus on very short-term price trends, the reasoning is more elusive. Markets invariably overreact to news, both true and false. So every price movement on a daily basis is the result of new information, overreaction, and correction. This is why, when a lot of information is available, prices tend to be more volatile than when all is quiet. Price movement confuses traders because they focus on the short-term chaotic movement of price, and on the reaction and overreaction to each and every change. In the futures market, change is not only specific to the industry in which a futures contract resides; geopolitical events also affect prices directly, with short-term overreaction followed by corrections in prices.

What this means for futures traders is that economic events—

the fundamentals of the market—are known to be all-important. But focus invariably goes to the price movement itself, which is technical in nature (see Chapter 7). However, if you understand the battle between supply and demand, you can better appreciate how and why prices change as they do. First, it makes sense to step back and look at the longer-term trends covering a month or more; or to look at futures price trends over a full year to understand how markets evolve and change. The day-to-day information is entirely technical and chaotic and cannot be used reliably to anticipate where prices are going next.

Second, if you understand how supply and demand works, your analysis of price trends will be more sensible. For example, one technical trend occurs when a price gaps, meaning that the opening price in today's session is higher or lower than the trading range of the previous session. A *series* of gaps usually leads to a retracement in price; this is a technical reality, but the law of supply and demand explains why it occurs.

The number of traders on both the long and the short side limit both supply and demand. So a sudden and unexpected movement in price occurs due to some change or perception of change, followed by a correcting movement in the opposite direction. For example, the March 2008 contract for coffee exhibited several gaps during the months of September and October, as highlighted in Figure 6-1.

Notice the prominent price gaps on the way up. Also notice that prices then retreat to fill in those gaps. This common pattern is normally thought of as a technical trend, but in fact it is caused by the law of supply and demand. In this situation, price rose on the perception among traders that coffee prices were at bargain levels. As a result, buying activity accelerated, creating the price gaps. But as the trend topped out, all of the traders who were going into the coffee futures contract were already in. There were no more buyers to continue driving the price higher. So price retreated to fill in those gaps. This is an illustration of the finite nature of supply and demand. Traders tend to believe that trends are potentially infinite and may continue without regard to supply and demand. But reality does not work in this way.

Later in the coffee contract, notice how prices begin edging

FIGURE 6.1. COFFEE—MARCH CONTRACT

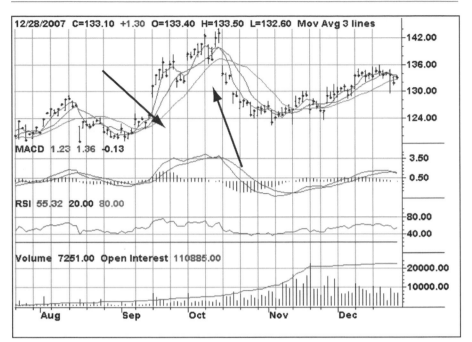

Source: Charts provided courtesy of TradingCharts.com: http//futures.tradingcharts.com; created with SuperCharts by Omega Research © 1997.

upward (November and December), accompanied by a spike in volume. This is a different trend, reflecting the rolling of previous contracts into the March contract. This is a "normal" trend because older contracts are replaced as a matter of course several times per year. So a distinction has to be made between price movement caused by aberrations in supply and demand (such as the price peak and retreat in October) versus the trend created by the predictable rolling out of older contracts into newer ones (as seen in November and December).

Futures markets are very much affected by market-level supply and demand, and this is very directly reflected in price. Beyond the action and overreaction of traders within the market, production levels, imports and exports, and changes in the basic market itself affect prices. For example, as interest has grown in ethanol fuel, the price of corn has risen. As a consequence, this affected both cattle and energy prices. Trends in agriculture, mining, housing, and even weather further affect futures prices. The national debt of many countries, inflation, and inventories of many products also affect the broad range of financial futures.

▧ Essential Economic Data

Supply and demand serves as a basic principle of how markets operate. The price movement of any product is a direct result of changes in supply and demand. However, many additional market indices based on economic trends also affect futures prices. These include:

Consumer Price Index (CPI), the index of prices used by the federal government and tracked by the Bureau of Labor Statistics (www.bls.gov). CPI is calculated using a weighted variety of goods and services, including food, energy, apparel, housing, transportation, and medical care. The "core CPI" includes necessities only, such as food and energy, a further distinction of the cost of living and its trend. Virtually all of the CPI components involve and rely upon commodities of one or more kinds.

Gross Domestic Product (GDP), which is the total value of all goods and services produced in the United States. It is usually expressed on a *per capita* basis, and implies changes in demand for commodities and their price changes. The Bureau of Economic Analysis tracks and reports on GDP and many other economic trends (www.bea.gov/national/index.htm#gdp).

Balance of trade, or the net difference between goods exported from the United States and goods imported from other countries. In the past, exports outpaced imports; but beginning in the 1970s, the balance of trade changed and since then, imports have outpaced exports. The U.S. Census Bureau tracks balance of trade by country (www.census.gov/foreign-trade/balance). To view annual trade balances on a detailed chart, go to www.census.gov/foreign-trade/statistics/historical/gands.txt.

Federal Funds Interest Rate, the interest rate set by the Federal Open Market Committee (www.federalreserve.gov/FOMC), the arm of the Federal Reserve System established to regulate or change interest rates. The Federal Funds rate is the rate banks charge one another. The Fed raises or lowers rates based on economic trends. For example, at the end of 2000, the rate was at 6.5%. However, after 9/11, the Fed lowered the rate to 1.75%, and two years later lowered it down to 1.00%. The rate then rose for several years, and was reduced once again in 2007. A summary of the Federal Funds rate for 10 years is shown in Figure 6-2.

EIA Inventory Level, the level of oil reserves in the United States. The Energy Information Administration (www.eia .doe.gov), part of the Department of Energy, releases weekly

FIGURE 6.2. FEDERAL FUNDS RATE, YEAR-END LEVEL

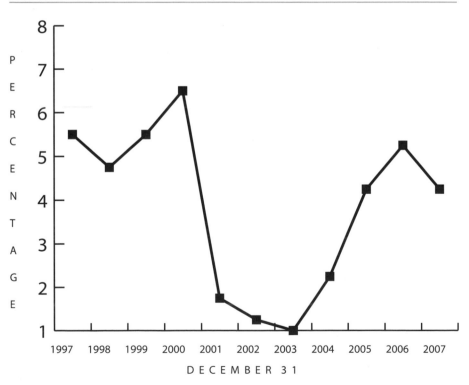

Source: Federal Reserve, www.federalreserve.gov/fomc/fundsrate.htm.

summaries of crude oil supply levels, including production, refining, and changes in current inventory levels. These reports affect the price of oil sector futures. A reduced inventory represents lower supply levels and creates upward pressure on petroleum product prices.

Non-Farm Payrolls, a summary of employment trends. It excludes agricultural, government, household employees, and workers in the not-for-profit industry. It includes salaried employees in U.S.-based businesses, or about 80% of total employment. The Bureau of Labor Statistics compiles the statistics as CES—current employment statistics—(www .bls.gov/ces). Information comes out on the first Friday of each month, reflecting changes in employment levels. Higher employment levels are positive economic trends, and the increases in the futures market from 2003 through 2007 reflect employment increases every month. By the end of 2007, employment was at 95%, considered "full employment" by most economists.

U.S. Dollar Value, or the value relative to other currencies. While U.S. dollar futures trade as a separate futures contract, the dollar has more significance than its relative value. The dollar is an international currency in many respects, and directly affects commodity prices, notably imports such as oil, coffee, cocoa, and metals like copper. Changes in the dollar's exchange rate have ramifications for many other futures trends. To view the relative value of the U.S. dollar throughout its history, go to www.measuringworth.com/calculators/compare.

WTI Crude Oil Price, the West Texas Intermediate benchmark. This widely followed price level for crude oil, traded on NYMEX, is described by the Department of Energy at http://tonto.eia.doe.gov/ask/crude_types1.html. It is a high-quality crude oil, also called Texas Light Sweet crude oil. Its price trend often is compared to North Sea Brent Crude.

Reuters/Jeffries CRB Index, the longest established commodity index, used as a benchmark for the entire industry as well

as an important economic indicator. The index (www.crb
trader.com/crbindex) began in 1957 and was given its current name in 2005 (also see www.jefferies.com/cositemgr
.pl/html/ProductsServices/SalesTrading/Commodities/Reu
tersJefferiesCRB/index.shtml). Many market watchers consider this index the industry benchmark, similar to the view
held among stock market analysts of the DJIA or the S&P
500.

Purchasing Managers' Index (PMI), a composite index of U.S.
manufacturing activity. The Institute for Supply Management (www.ism.ws—click on the link "ISM Report on
Business") publishes the PMI on the first business day of
each month, and it is important because many commodities
are used in manufacturing activities, notably energy.

London Gold Fixing, a measurement of the only commodity
with monetary value and a monetary role (thus crucial to
the financial futures sector as well as to a broad range of
commodities). London Fixing (www.goldfixing.com) reflects spot gold prices and serves as a benchmark. The London Fixing sets a single gold price internationally, with a
new fix set twice per business day. Metals dealers and gold
futures traders track the trends in this benchmark very
closely.

Many additional economic indicators provide data for specific
segments of the economy or for focused commodity trading. The
previous selection represents a broad overview of essential economic reports and data available nationally.

▪ Fundamentals of Other Countries

Understanding the basic economic fundamentals for the United
States is a requirement for futures trading. However, in the global
economy that continues to emerge, it is becoming increasingly necessary to also track economic indicators for other countries, regions, and even globally. However, this is a problem because
reporting standards are not always the same as those well-known
standards in the United States.

As a starting point, track basic economic indicators for the major economic forces in the world. This is valuable because it allows you to compare U.S. levels of indicators to those of trade partners and rivals. Check www.allcountries.org/uscensus/1367 _selected_international_economic_indicators_by_country.html to view some basic country-by-country comparisons of economic data, such as the ratio of gross fixed capital formation to GDP, and the rate of savings to personal disposable income. These data provide some level of comparison and provide trend lines for development of international comparisons. That is quite useful if you want to invest in futures that emphasize or focus on a particular country or region, or that dominate a specific futures product.

To view economic data for specific countries, check the Web site for the CIA's *World Factbook*, at https://www.cia.gov/library/publications/the-world-factbook/index.html. By selecting a country at the top of the page, you are able to go to a specific link. For example, if you enter "China" and then click on the link for "Economy," an overview is provided along with the key economic data. The information is quite extensive. You can repeat the same steps for any country.

Another valuable site for worldwide economic data is the World Bank, an agency with 185 member countries providing financial support to developing nations. On its Web site, it links to economic data, at www.worldbank.org/data/countrydata/countrydata.html. Note the selection box, defaulting to "world." You can enter any country in this selection box and find economic data immediately. Profiles of countries and regions are also provided just below that first section. On the left, you can link to "key statistics" and locate a variety of information in greater detail. For anyone who wants to research global economic trends, this is a valuable site.

The online version of *The Economist* is a great source for in-depth descriptions of economic conditions in various countries. Link to www.economist.com/countries/China/profile.cfm?folder = Profile-Economic%20 to see a report about China, for example. If you replace the area of the address /China/ with the name of another country—for example, /India/—you can get additional reports. Especially valuable are the many links this site provides. For example, it gives you Web site links to Chinese government links, the Xinhua

News Agency, the *People's Daily* newspaper, *China Daily*, *China Perspectives*, and the Web site for China Today, an online news, travel, and information service. Related links include one to many Chinese Web sites, and the Brookings Institution's collection of China-related articles. These links can make anyone an expert on China, or any other country, without needing to search far and wide. The link for India provides a range of Web links as well, including a directory of Indian government Web sites, *Hindustan Times*, *The Times of India*, *The Telegraph*, the National Stock Exchange, the Securities and Exchange Board of India, Reserve Bank, Centre for Monitoring the Indian Economy, All Indian Radio, and Confederation of Indian Industry (CII)—a nongovernment organization (NGO) representing Indian business interest abroad. You can find similar pages and links for many countries on this site, providing you with a vast range of economic research.

The sites listed previously all help to round out your ability to develop independent research; and your own online searches for more specific information can add to the list.

Problems with International Economic Data

The basic assumption made about virtually all forms of data is that the information is reliable. This is not always the case. In the United States, stock investors have relied on the independence of the financial audit to ensure that companies were telling the truth to stockholders. As the experience of Enron and many other companies has demonstrated, this basic assumption may be flawed. Even today, with significant legislative reforms at the federal level and increased regulatory oversight, the question of auditing objectivity is unresolved. Auditing firms continue to perform billions of dollars worth of non-audit work, often for the same clients they audit. This glaring conflict of interest makes the point: You cannot rely on information provided by SEC filings, audited financial statements, or annual reports.

Now consider how more complex this issue is when you are dealing with foreign countries and with companies based in those countries. In order to invest in futures, you should be able to rely on international economic information. But in so many cases, you have to take such information with a bit of suspicion. The case of the biggest economic rival to the United States, which is China, demonstrates this point.

China's economic reports leave out a lot of important information. For example, the overall government debt of China does not include *non-performing loans (NPLs)*. These are debts of *state-owned enterprises (SOEs)*, which are hybrid organizations combining some features of free-market capitalism and some of Communist state-run business. The official Chinese state banking system states NPLs at 25% of Chinese GDP; but the real number could be as high as 40%.[1]

The rate of future defaults on these kinds of loans may be quite high, so overall the degree of Chinese state-level debt is probably understated, and if the uncollectible loans were reported by Western standards, Chinese budget deficits may be far higher than reported as well. Even though the official reporting of these loans is separate from government debt, these loans really are a form of what would be the equivalent of Western-style national debt; if that were underreported in the United States, it would severely affect economic reporting.

Economic reporting from China is also not on the same level with U.S. indicators due to the problems of unemployment. In the United States, unemployment is subdivided by industry and economic sector, and economic reporting reports unemployment on a national basis. But in China, there are three unemployment-related "sectors" or types:

Urban unemployment, which has run at an average of 3% to 4%.

Rural unemployment, which also includes underemployment because so many agricultural workers and farmers are unemployed for a substantial portion of the year. This makes rural unemployment far higher than any reported totals, because the partial-year unemployment (underemployment) is not included. About 75% of rural families own land, but most of those are extremely small plots, and in fact, they are too small to sustain the needs of the owner's family year-round.

Unemployed former state workers, a large segment and an aging portion of the workforce; this is especially problematical because, under the old Communist-led system, state workers were guaranteed work. Today, work is simply not available for all. From 1997 through 2001, 24 million state workers were laid off, part of a massive transition in the Chinese economy to a free-market model. This has drained the Chinese welfare system and increased the growing debt as well as the unemployment numbers.

Even employed Chinese workers have problems if they are working in the SOE sector. Many are not paid regularly, with delayed paychecks extending out to nearly a full year in some instances. Meanwhile, the newer non-SOE sector is creating many new jobs and offering better wages as well. The government is going through a multiyear effort to move SOE employees into non-state jobs through its Urban Reemployment Center (URC) program. But progress is slow, and urban unemployment is profound.

Another confusing economic statistic from China involves trends in average income. In fact, income varies considerably by region within China. Slow growth in predominantly rural parts of the country have been caused partly by massive industrialization in coastal and southern regions. But adding to the income disparity is a concentration of SOEs in those rural areas under the old-style system. Thus, current employment numbers are quite weak in rural regions compared to those in the urban and industrialized areas.

To look at the economic trends including GDP, employment and income, it appears that the Chinese economy is moving upward at breathtaking speed. But this does not fully account for the large problems of rural poverty in northern provinces, which has remained unchanged for many years. A long-term migration away from these rural areas and into industrialized regions has created additional problems of growing urban unemployment (especially among unskilled and undereducated rural transplants), congestion, pollution, and the replacement of rural poverty with urban poverty.

A final consideration in any comparative economic analysis is corruption. While this is slowly improving, traditionally corrupt traditions in both government and private companies have been a huge problem, more so in SOEs than elsewhere. The slow replacement of SOEs with a free-market economy is predicted as a major force that will eventually do away with much of the corruption in Chinese business, as one observer noted:

> A great part of the problem of corruption is tied to the existence of big state-owned economic sectors, not only the government bureaucracy and political structure. Therefore, the privatization of the SOEs and reforms of other state-owned institutions will be one of the key factors in reducing corruption.[2]

The disparity between regions further complicates long-term analysis of China. China has a two-pronged problem: There are many mouths to feed, and a vast migration into the urban areas is occurring without pause. This trend may add to employment and GDP while reducing overall poverty, *assuming* that the Chinese economy can continue to produce enough jobs. But at the same time, unemployment is rising among unskilled urban workers while shortages are found among trained and skilled ones.

This is seen in the fact that low-wage factory and manufacturing workers are abundant; but Chinese government and industry has not invested in skilled employment training, such as technology and technological manufacturing.

As far as a study of the futures market is concerned, remember that China is the second largest energy consumer in the world, after the United States. But China already is experiencing power shortages. Blackouts and brownouts occur in the large cities on a regular basis, and sections of industrial cities close early several times per month because energy reserves are simply not available. This trend points to a limiting factor on growth of the Chinese economy. If energy resources cannot keep up with expanded industrial activity in China, that alone could cause the Chinese economy to flatten out. Much research is being conducted on alternative fuels like clean-burning coal, liquefaction, nuclear, and hydrogen-based fuels. Many of these are less polluting than coal and oil, and potentially more affordable. The trend may point the way to great potential in futures trading, although new technology invariably takes longer than anyone would like.

The examination of China and its unique problems is an example of how and why you have to make comparisons cautiously. In the futures market, all economies are distinct and separate, so like-kind comparisons are elusive. The same warning applies to the study of any country. If you focus on the futures market prominent in a particular kind of commodity, remember that the numbers should not be assumed to be comparable to the reports from the U.S. government.

Fundamental analysis of futures trading is complex because economic data can be conflicting and unclear. You cannot always know how developing economic trends are going to affect the specific value of a futures contract. One solution to this is to make regular comparisons between economic data and trading trends. You may also find additional confirming information by combining fundamental analysis with technical analysis. This is the study of price trends and ranges. Chapter 7 deals with the subject of technical analysis of the futures market.

■ Notes

1. Nicholas R. Lardy, *China's Unfinished Economic Revolution* (Washington, DC: Brookings Institute, 1998).
2. Fan Gang, "Reform and Development: The Dual-Transformation of China," in *China: Enabling a New Era of Changes* ed. Pamela C. M. Mar and Frank-Jürgen Richter (Singapore: John Wiley—Asia, 2003).

TECHNICAL ANALYSIS
OF FUTURES

n all forms of investing, you may adopt either a fundamental or a technical approach. The fundamental approach relies on the hard numbers. In the stock market, that means tracking a company's financial statements and looking for trends. Those trends reflect quality of management, competition within a sector, and market demand. In the futures market, the fundamental approach relies more on economic trends, and is somewhat removed from actual price action. The difficulty in the futures market is equating fundamental trends to specific price movement. Furthermore, the trends in one area affect prices in another; for example, as energy prices rise, the prices of agricultural commodities are affected directly.

The technical approach focuses primarily on price action. In evaluating supply and demand, you need to be aware of two different and dissimilar aspects of that basic economic theory. First is the economic supply and demand. Markets drive the cost of any product, and that is reflected in trading interest and price direction of the underlying commodity. This is the *fundamental* version. But there is also a *technical* version of the supply and demand interaction. Economic trends affect prices, but they also vary by market supply and demand, which is based more on perception than on any economic reality. For example, if the belief dominates that energy prices are going to rise next year, you will see speculation driving up the price of energy futures contracts. When you watch financial news programs and see the current "price of oil," that is not what you are paying at the pump. It is what the price traders are currently trading for oil futures contracts. So any unrest in the Middle East is going to drive prices up; and as those prices rise, other commodities follow suit. The technical supply and demand is a forward-looking phenomenon whereas the fundamental version is based on past and current economic fact.

In the technical analysis of futures, the concept on contrarian trading is often very popular. In this theory, you go against the majority, because you believe that the majority is usually wrong, acting too late, or overreacting to current information. A contrarian buys when everyone else is selling, and sells when everyone else is buying. It is usually more complex than simply tracking rising or falling prices. Contrarians are likely to also track advancing and declining trends, volume and open interest, and market trends in related commodities.

The smart way to analyze futures trading is by combining both fundamental and technical approaches, using all the useful indicators you can find to confirm, contradict, or add to the body of information. The following are some of the essential technical points worth remembering.

Charting Basics: Tracking Price Behavior

The chart is the essential visual tool of the technician. Charts show the trading pattern at once. The difficult part is interpreting the chart and deciding what it means. Depending on how the pattern is evolving, you can interpret a price chart in many possible ways.

For example, Figure 7-1 shows the April contract for lean hogs for the first few trading days of January 2008.

Note the strong downward price trend, marked with the straight lines. How do you interpret this? For the technician, this pattern presents a problem of interpretation. One explanation is that the price trend is *clearly* downward and is likely to continue in that direction. However, note that after the bottom of the down

FIGURE 7.1. LEAN HOGS—APRIL CONTRACT DAILY CHART

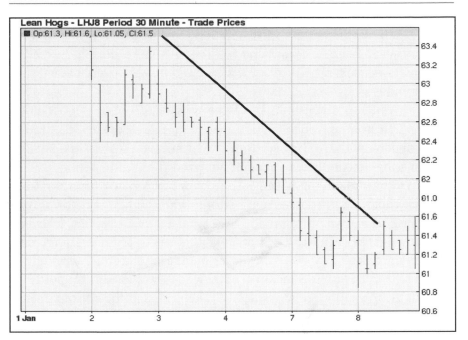

Source: Charts provided courtesy of TradingCharts.com: http://futures.tradingcharts.com; created with SuperCharts by Omega Research © 1997.

trend, price pauses and is followed by periods of very narrow trading. Then the price begins rising. This could mean that price has reached the bottom of the short-term trend and is about to begin rising again.

Among the charting techniques you can use, one is the tracking of trends by size, shape, and duration of movement in one direction. Using the technique known as swing trading, traders like to move in and out of positions in a two- to five-day sequence. Using chart patterns to identify tops and bottoms, a combination of trend duration and reversal signals sets the buy and sell timing.

Swing traders identify uptrends as a series of trading periods consisting of consecutive higher highs, offset by higher lows. A downtrend consists of a consecutive series of lower lows offset by lower highs. In the figure, swing traders will recognize a likely bottom in the price trend based on the downward movement toward the end of the visible pattern. As the price levels begin to rise following this, swing traders would signal a setup to go long in the contract, or to close out their shorts.

However, another interpretation may observe that the upward offset at the end of the chart is nothing more than a correcting movement filling in a strong decline; and that the overall downward trend is likely to resume.

You can argue both points of view in this case. The solution in determining which version makes more sense is to look to the fundamentals. An fxstreet.com Dow Jones newswire story explaining the activity on this market analyzed the trend, stating in part, "Despite continued negative subsequent cash news, futures gradually floated up from session bottoms with the help of short covering."[1] This was a reference to several factors affecting lean hog prices. The cash trend was notably weak and it appeared at the time of the news story that short covering caused the short-term uptick in the price levels. So many traders who had opened short positions at the top of the trend wanted to take profits at the bottom, meaning they needed to enter "buy to close" orders. In all markets, short covering is a closing of positions, but it often has the effect of looking and acting the same as buying pressure. You might conclude from this that the apparent upward move is a momentary effect caused by short covering, meaning that there is no sound reason to believe that prices are on the rebound. Additionally, livestock prices were in a weakening trend during this period, so there does not appear to be any impetus for a dramatic turnaround or change in the price direction.

The technician reviews charts in an attempt to perform this kind of analysis. One of the most important aspects of chart analysis is observation of the trading range, or the space between the top and bottom. In the previous chart, the trading range maintained approximately the same distance from top to bottom, even while the general price level declined. This was a one- to two-point spread, not a lot of change. However, it is significant to observe that the consistency of breadth remained unchanged over the four-day period. A technician may interpret this as a sign of continuing low volatility even in conditions of falling prices.

In comparison, not all trading ranges are so reliable in terms of breadth, or the distance between high and low prices. For example,

Figure 7-2 shows the April contract in natural gas. This pattern is far more volatile and difficult to predict. Chart watchers face this dilemma constantly. A very low-volatility chart is easy to predict, but small price movement reduces trading opportunities. And high-volatility charts present greater chances for short-term profits, but they are more difficult to predict based on trading patterns.

In the case of the natural gas contract, three short-term trading patterns—all rather strong—are experienced. The first and third are uptrends, and the second is a correcting downtrend. Where will it go next? The point difference during this period is not tremendous, but the volatility itself implies some additional likely problems in the market. This is where the fundamentals and the current news come into the picture. This price pattern emerged during a period of high volatility for all energy futures, augmented by rumors of recession, unrest in the Middle East, and consumer worries about inflation (which were at least partially blamed on rising oil prices across the board).

FIGURE 7.2. NATURAL GAS—APRIL CONTRACT DAILY CHART

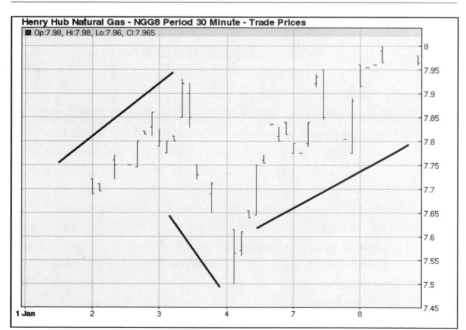

Source: Charts provided courtesy of TradingCharts.com: http//futures.tradingcharts.com; created with SuperCharts by Omega Research © 1997.

The tops and bottoms of trading ranges are very difficult to identify in the short-term chart for natural gas, because trading moves all over the chart. In situations like this, it makes sense to also review longer-term charts to view the larger trend, and to help identify potential seasonal effects as well, not to mention current news headlines and a summary of the economic report.

The technical approach is based on the important concept of *support and resistance*. This is a reference to the lowest and highest price levels in the current trading range. Support is the lowest price at which buyers and sellers agree to exchange contracts, and resistance is the highest agreed-upon price. As a general rule, prices tend to remain within established support and resistance borders, and this is significant for three reasons:

1. *The support and resistance levels define volatility.* The nature of the trading range defines the very level of volatility. That range, defined in turn by the established support and resistance price points, is expected to hold unless a major change occurs.

2. *As the trading range narrows or widens, technicians anticipate future price changes as well.* This all-important trend reveals and anticipates new directions in the near future. Changes in volatility, represented by narrowing and widening ranges, is a further indication of pending change.

3. *Any attempt to break through support or resistance is important, whether it fails or succeeds.* If price approaches support twice or more and then retreats, technicians expect price levels to rise in response. The "failed" breakout below support shows selling weakness, and that implies buying strength. The opposite is true on the top: If price approaches the resistance level two or more times but fails to break through, it implies buying weakness, and prices are expected to fall shortly afterwards. These failed attempts are seen in technical patterns like double or triple tops and bottoms. The head and shoulders pattern is another, with three rises to resistance followed by a price retreat. This is considered a failed breakout pattern at resistance. A reverse head and shoulders shows the same pattern, but at support.

A successful breakout may imply one of two price trends. First is a momentary breakout, in which price levels are expected to fill and retreat to previously established trading range levels. Second is a strong price movement resulting in establishing a new trading range. The inclusion of gaps in trading price levels helps technicians to interpret breakout patterns and to determine what they mean.

Pattern Recognition and Interpretation

Price movement adopts distinct patterns. Technical analysts have noticed that these patterns often anticipate price weakness or strength in coming periods. By looking for pattern changes, technical analysts also believe that they can time their trades to take advantage of momentary market aberrations. There is some support for this. Remember, markets tend to overreact to news and information. In spite of the long-term price direction, price action within a single day or over a few days tends to be chaotic; and movement is likely to consist of movement in one direction, offset by countermovement the other way, an unending series of erratic movements, corrections, and subsequent movements.

The existence of support and resistance as the boundaries of established trading ranges provides a clear and definitive area where trading is expected to occur. Sudden price movements even within trading ranges can be significant, especially if those movements approach the boundaries or violate them. And when it comes to pattern recognition, it is significant that a trading range is not so much an exact price level, but a range of trading breadth.

For example, if a particular future is trading between 8 and 11, its breadth is three points. As long as the price remains within those ranges, the price levels are fairly predictable even if there is a lot of back-and-forth action. But in other futures contracts, a three-point range may exist in a contract that is moving up or down in price. The example shown in Figure 7-1 demonstrated how this works. The breadth remained very constant even as prices fell.

The trend within a trading range—unchanged, rising, or falling—is called the price channel. Traders like predictability, so as long as the support and resistance levels are easily spotted, it is

comforting to accept the premise that the range itself, or at least
the point spread in the breadth, is going to remain constant. Chan-
nels can take a number of shapes and sizes, sometimes rising and
at other times falling. A momentary sideways price movement may
arise as a rest during a longer-term uptrend or downtrend as well.
This pattern is also called a rectangle, because it forms that shape
with resistance on the top, support on the bottom, and the sides
consisting of a start and finish. For example, the propane monthly
chart shown in Figure 7-3 establishes an overall upward price
movement, but with two periods of relatively sideways-moving
trading. This example of support and resistance occurs often as
part of a longer-term price pattern.

The channel is simply the price movement within the range,

FIGURE 7.3. PROPANE—MONTHLY CHART

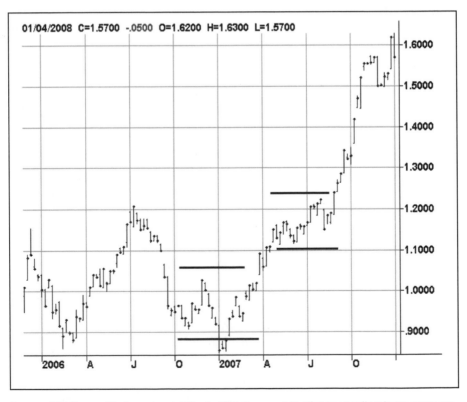

Source: Charts provided courtesy of TradingCharts.com: http//futures.tradingcharts.com; created with SuperCharts by Omega Research © 1997.

and that may be sideways, upward or downward in direction. Another significant pattern is the triangle. This is a trading pattern where the breadth of the range narrows or widens. For example, the weekly chart for corn futures demonstrates a triangle pattern as shown in Figure 7-4.

In two instances on this chart, the pattern widens in anticipation of a strong price movement. This does not mean that the pattern is always going to occur in the same manner, but it is one indication of expanding breadth, which also translates to expanded buyer/seller exchange.

The patterns and variations on those patterns are among many tools technicians use. As chartists—those who time trades based on chart patterns—futures traders have to act quickly because the market may change within a single day. The rapid volume of trading in some commodities makes chart analysis elusive. Looking at very long-term trends is unreliable as well, given the short-term life of each specific contract. However, when applied to daily price

FIGURE 7.4. CORN CONTRACT—WEEKLY

Source: Charts provided courtesy of TradingCharts.com: http//futures.tradingcharts.com; created with SuperCharts by Omega Research © 1997.

movements, the trader who employs chart patterns to assist in the timing of trades may be able to anticipate developing price movement.

Trend Lines and Moving Averages

Traders follow channel patterns seeking information to time buy and sell decisions. In stocks, long-term trends are granted a lot of credibility, because companies are permanent and stock trends do tend to follow distinct overall tendencies. For futures, though, the short-term trend is more likely to be followed. While overall futures prices are expected to trend in a particular way, the action that really matters is what occurs in the past month and what is going to occur in the next month.

An example of a strong uptrend can be seen in the long-term monthly chart for gold futures, as shown in Figure 7-5.

Note that the uptrend occurred over several years, and was very strong. Toward the end of 2007, the gold price rose even more strongly. This augments the rate of increase, but should also concern gold futures traders. The likelihood of profit taking becomes stronger when prices jump so quickly, because the tendency is for price to retreat and fill in, at least in line with the established rate of change.

An uptrend in gold often reflects currency weakness. For example, during the same period that gold rose strongly, the U.S. dollar fell. Figure 7-6 shows the monthly dollar futures value.

From 1999 to 2001, the dollar actually rose, but since then it has fallen. After a brief rally in 2005, the decline took over once again. Thus, the long-term trend for the U.S. dollar is ever-greater weakness. Some traders view this as part of an ongoing trend that is expected to continue, while others expect a dollar rebound in the future. The point here, however, is to demonstrate the appearance of a downtrend over the long term. The fact that the downtrend lasted for so many years demonstrates how some futures trends develop and are sustained. The comparison between gold and currency values further shows how virtually all futures are connected to one another in some manner. Just as energy prices affect grain value (notably corn as a feed source as well as potential energy

FIGURE 7.5. GOLD—MONTHLY CHART

12/31/2007 C=834.9 +52.7 O=787.5 H=839.6 L=786.0

Source: Charts provided courtesy of TradingCharts.com: http//futures.tradingcharts.com; created with SuperCharts by Omega Research © 1997

source), gold and currency values also tend to move opposite of one another.

The rise or fall in a trend is rarely going to occur in a straight line. If you look at current charts, even for futures that are clearly midtrend, you will often find a back-and-forth price action. For example, prices will rise several points, then retreat, followed by another rise. This effect, called climbing the stairs, is common in both directions. Because buyers and sellers are constantly negotiating back and forth, the forces of supply and demand are rarely going to occur in one direction for very long, without offsetting movement in the opposite direction.

An aid to understanding trends is the moving average. In many charts, you find not only the periodic price action represented by vertical lines or boxes; but also one or more lines moving across the chart, representing moving averages.

FIGURE 7.6. U.S. DOLLAR MONTHLY CONTRACT

12/31/2007 C=76.70 +.53 O=75.97 H=77.88 L=75.61

Source: Charts provided courtesy of TradingCharts.com: http//futures.tradingcharts.com; created with SuperCharts by Omega Research © 1997.

A simple moving average is calculated by adding together the number of periods; and then dividing the total by the number. Each period's new moving average is calculated in the same way, adding new data and dropping off old data. Futures analysis often involves the combined use of 50-period and 200-period moving averages. With online charting, calculations do not have to be made, because they are performed automatically. Each period's moving average (MA) line represents the latest updated information.

A variation of the simple MA is called exponential moving average (EMA). This calculation is more complex, because it grants more weight to the latest information. Using EMA is justified because the latest information reflects more updated knowledge about the underlying commodity. So the move in the futures price may be granted greater weight due to its current importance.

The significance of MAs involves comparisons between the averages and the level of price. MAs are expected to follow price movements, because averages are lagging indicators of price. So if price falls beneath the MA, technical analysts believe this signals a downward trend, and the MA is expected to follow. The purpose of studying MA is to identify a lag time and anticipate likely price action based on how MA stands in comparison to current price levels.

MACD and RSI

Moving average certainly provides a revealing look at price movement and trend. A variation of this useful tool is called MACD, which summarizes the daunting name, Moving Average Convergence Divergence.

MACD converts MA into what technicians refer to as a "momentum oscillator." This is a type of indicator comparing earlier prices to more recent prices, with the purpose of judging how rapidly price is changing.

Any two moving averages can be used in MACD, although the most popular are 12-day and 26-day exponential moving averages. The so-called 12/26 MACD is studied by how close or far apart they are, as a means for determining the longer-term price trend. When the 12-day is higher than the 26-day MA, that is considered positive and anticipates that price is going to rise; and of course the opposite pattern implies that price is likely to fall. Taking this beyond the stationary comparison, when the two MAs are moving farther apart (diverging) or coming closer together (converging) the MACD is even more revealing. There are actually four possible MACD patterns:

1. The shorter-term MA is above the longer-term MA, and the two are diverging. This indicates strong upward momentum in price.
2. The shorter-term MA is above the longer-term MA, but the two are converging. This indicates that the rising price trend is becoming weaker.
3. The longer-term MA is above the shorter-term MA, and the two

are diverging. This indicates a strong downward momentum in price.

4. The longer-term MA is above the shorter-term MA, but the two are converging. This indicates that the falling price trend is becoming weaker.

MACD analysis can also involve the use of a signal line other than price. A third MA, for example, may add additional insight about a future contract's price strength or weakness. However, proximity to delivery date is going to affect MACD analysis as well. Remember, futures traders use a continuous rolling effect, meaning that current holdings are closed and replaced by later-expiring delivery dates. This also affects the price and may distort the apparent MACD. It may be accurate to observe that MACD for longer-spanning trends is more reliable than when it is applied against the current contract. MACD is popular to use for stock price analysis, given the longer-term nature of stocks. However, it is one more piece of the puzzle in technical analysis of futures.

A more reliable measure of price strength or weakness is the Relative Strength Index (RSI) of a futures contract. This indicator, like MACD, is a momentum oscillator because it is designed to measure and compare the price momentum in the contract. So using RSI, you can determine the speed of price change (momentum), and also derive a single-digit indicator comparing the strength of price increases with the strength of price decreases.

RSI is normally summarized on a futures chart (as well as MACD), to augment the reported price level and trend. The RSI calculation is a popular momentum oscillator and perhaps more applicable to futures contracts than the more oblique MACD. RSI compares recent price gains to price losses, and then converts the difference into a single value between zero and 100. The calculation is based on varying time frames, often 14 days. Most analysts consider a factor of 70 or higher to be the line defining when a futures contract is overbought; and use 30 or below as the point where the contract is undersold. So as a clear bullish (70 or higher) or bearish (30 or lower) signal, RSI is easily tracked and interpreted. As with all indices, it is valuable to track RSI over time. For example, if RSI is ranging between 50 and 65 consistently, and then spikes up to 75 for one or two days, that does not mean everything has changed. As long as RSI retreats to the midlevel factor, you can ignore the momentary spike. In comparison, if the RSI is gradually increasing and passes 70, remaining above that level, it is more likely that the futures contract is overbought at that point.

The fact that RSI ranges between zero and 100 implies that the midpoint between overbought and oversold is always 50. However, this can be misleading because short-term aberrations in trends can move RSI above or below that level frequently without violating the more obvious "above 70" and "below 30" criteria. This is especially true when you remember that all indicators have to also consider the relatively short-term delivery and the natural rolling out of one contract and into another.

For an example of an overbought futures contract, see the March 2008 propane contract summarized in Figure 7-7.

FIGURE 7.7. PROPANE—MARCH CONTRACT

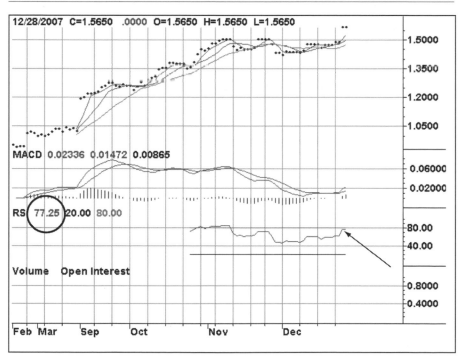

Source: Charts provided courtesy of TradingCharts.com: http//futures.tradingcharts.com; created with SuperCharts by Omega Research © 1997.

Prices rose strongly throughout the previous year, and then appeared to reach a resistance point between November and December. This would be difficult to interpret by itself. However, RSI had dipped into the midrange during exactly the same period, but toward the end actually rose above 70, settling at 77.25 by the end of December. Technicians tracking RSI would have noted this increase at the last half of December 2007 and concluded that the contract was overbought.

An example of a futures contract approaching oversold conditions was the March 2008 lumber contract, as shown in Figure 7-8.

Although the RSI remains above 30, note the trend. If RSI continues to fall as it did between August and December, chances are the contract would become oversold. RSI remains slightly above 30 for most of this period, but toward the end had fallen to 31. Any

FIGURE 7.8. LUMBER—MARCH CONTRACT

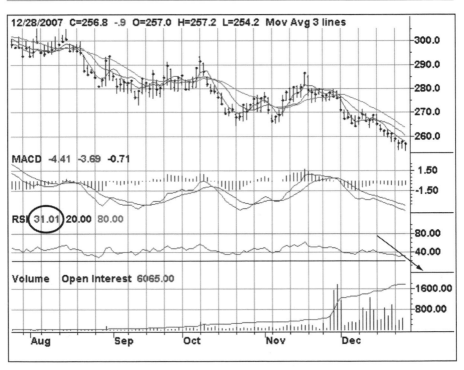

additional decline would signal that the price had reached bottom, and would level out and rise. In fact, the same contract continued its decline and by January 10, RSI had fallen dramatically, as shown in Figure 7-9.

Note that the price decline continued in the 10 days since the prior chart, but RSI fell to 15.79, a clear sign that the contract was oversold. Because RSI involves a single point value, determining the trend is simple, and the price rise or decline is given greater meaning, helping traders time their decisions.

▓ Volume, Open Interest, Bollinger, Elliott, and Stochastic

You will notice that in addition to MACD and RSI, charts contain both open interest and volume. The open interest is the number of

FIGURE 7.9. LUMBER—MARCH CONTRACT (AS OF JANUARY 10, 2008)

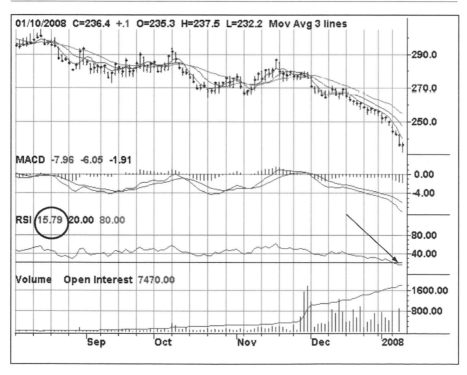

currently outstanding and active contracts; and volume, shown at the bottom of the complete chart, shows the number of trades occurring in each reported period.

A "unit" of open interest involves a buyer and a seller, so when the two sides come together, they reside on each side of a single contract. The trend in open interest is interesting to watch. Naturally, as delivery nears, open interest is expected to decline when traders roll positions into later contracts. Volume trends may also anticipate pending price movement. Referring back to the March lumber contract in Figure 7-9, for example, you see that volume spiked at the beginning of December and prices (and RSI) both fell sharply throughout the month of December and into January.

Volume is important because it indicates the level of interest in the contract. The lumber contract is a good example of this. Notice that volume was quite low until December, and following the spike, volume remained much higher than it had been previously. Either buying or selling activity can lead the level of interest in a futures contract. In the case of March lumber, sellers were clearly generating interest as both price and RSI fell on heavy volume. That situation is referred to as *distribution*, meaning that sellers are in control. Long positions closing drive the exceptional volume. For those with short positions in the contract, the deterioration in price translates to profits. When buyers drive volume, it is called *accumulation*, meaning that traders view the contract as desirable. The buying demand drives up the price.

Three final but important technical indicators worth mentioning are Bollinger, Elliott, and Stochastics. Although these sound like a law firm, they are not. Bollinger Bands are indicators used to compare futures contract volatility. There are three price bands in the analysis. The primary band is in the middle and consists of a simple moving average of price. The second (upper) and third (lower) bands are calculated to show how much deviation occurs from the average price on both upside and downside. When prices are volatile, Bollinger Bands expand away from the primary trend, and when prices are more stable, the bands contract. As prices get closer to the upper band, it indicates that the contract is becoming oversold. (It is also productive to study Bollinger Bands in conjunction with RSI to see whether these two indicators confirm the indicated significance.) And as the price gets closer to the lower band, it indicates an oversold condition. Bollinger Bands are excellent confirming indicators.

The Elliott Wave is an indicator involving a series of waves in one direction, used to spot long-term trends. This indicator is probably more applicable to stock price analysis than to futures, but many futures technicians use Elliott Wave studies as a further confirmation of RSI and other indicators.

The *stochastic* is a measurement of oscillation like so many other technical indicators. Price volatility is a defining predictive value in future contracts. A stochastic measurement compares current price to the daily trading range. The idea behind this is the belief that price tends to follow the established trend; so if an uptrend dominates, price tends to close closer to the upper trading range, for example. However, when a trend has been going on for some time, you may notice a weakening in the stochastic strength. This anticipates a slowing down of the trend and perhaps a reversal in the near future. It is more esoteric than indicators like RSI and the simple observation of price movement over recent trading periods. Few people would need extra help in understanding the direction of the trend in the March lumber contract, for example. However, a stochastic study could point to a slowing down in the downtrend itself.

You may find any number of technical indicators to help compare and study price action in a futures contract. However, because futures are going to exist for only a limited period of time (in comparison to stocks, which do not have delivery deadlines), so many technical indicators developed for stock analysis may not be applicable or as informative when applied to futures.

The next chapter explains in detail a final method of reaching the market—trading in options on futures. Options provide an interesting alternative to other methods of trading, and make the entire futures market accessible on a highly leveraged basis.

Notes

1. Theopolis Waters, "Pork Futures, Hogs Advance," Dow Jones Newswires, January 8, 2008. (reprinted at FXstreet.com).

THE LEVERAGED APPROACH: OPTIONS ON FUTURES

The complexity of futures trading is, for most traders, best managed by using indices and ETFs. Direct trading is expensive and involves many risks most people do not want to accept. In addition, the futures contract is an intangible derivative of the underlying commodity or asset. Most futures traders never intend to accept or make delivery of the actual product, but are only speculating on the changing price levels.

Complicating matters even more, you can buy or sell options on futures. This is actually a derivative on a derivative, which is a complex step beyond most people's interest level. For those who want to examine the entire range of possible methods for reaching and studying the futures market, options open up some interesting possibilities, involving leverage of your money, reduced risk exposure, and added hedging possibilities. The ability to trade options on futures is a relatively new idea. The Chicago Board of Trade first introduced it in 1982, when such options were first allowed on Treasury bond futures contracts. Since then, the range of futures contracts on which options can be written is broad, and today traders are able to find many avenues for futures speculation and hedging with the use of options.

You leverage capital buying and selling options, because the option value (called the premium) is a small percentage of the full futures contract price. Just as the futures contract is a small portion of the underlying commodity, you reduce your capital even more by trading in options on those same futures. This is the epitome of leverage.

In most cases, added leverage also means more risk. But with options, the risk level really depends on whether you are long or short on a futures contract. The risk of short options can be considerable if the price takes off in the underlying commodity. Traders who would want to short the commodity think the price is going down. But with options, you can actually bet on the downside with a long position, and at the same time limit your capital exposure. The elegance of option trading is that it allows you to pick a trading strategy that is perfectly suited to your own risk tolerance level.

The following sections explain the basic attributes and definitions of options trading. For those readers familiar with options on stock or indices, an important distinction has to be made. With listed stock options, every option is related to 100 shares of the underlying stock. However, with futures, the contract value is different for each commodity. So you have to make sure that you know how many contracts you are involved with before determining whether the current price level of the option is attractive or not—and whether the risk level is acceptable if and when you *sell* options.

Options on futures are certainly interesting in the sense that their use can open the doors to many variables on trading. Even if you limit your trading activity to options on futures-based ETFs or index funds, options expand your potential market exposure while providing many hedging possibilities. Throughout this chapter, the examples used for option trades and strategies are focused on trades in futures ETFs and indices. This is the most likely venue for futures trading most readers are going to use. Thus, it is logical to also assume that the interest level is going to be focused on option trades for those pooled products. References to an option's "underlying security" can refer to a specific futures contract, but it is more likely that the security will be a fund comprised of futures contracts. Option examples will be based on the tracking index

GSCI Commodity Indexed Fund (GSG) and the oil ETF, United States Oil Fund (USO), as of the close of business on January 11, 2008. (Note: Although share values change continuously, the fixed point in time for these selections remain valid on a relative basis. Given the price levels and time element of option trading, you can accurately assess option values based on these examples.)

Types of Options

The first step in understanding options is to master the terminology in this specialized market. Most traders not familiar with options think they are complex and high risk. But this is not the case. The most important feature of the options market is that each trader is able to select a specific risk level, based on what kinds of options are used, and whether they are long or short.

Options are intangible contractual rights, much like futures contracts. They have a finite life and their value is based strictly on how futures contract prices change. There are two kinds of options, *calls* and *puts*. A call grants its buyer the right, but not the requirement, to purchase a specified number of futures contracts. This right has to be exercised within a specified time frame (before expiration date), and occurs at a fixed price, called the strike. Of course, if you buy a call, you do not have to buy those futures contracts. If their value rises, you can sell the call at a profit. Remembering this distinction between the two kinds of options is imperative to developing specific strategies.

A put is the opposite of a call. It grants its owner the right, but not the requirement, to sell a specified number of futures contracts at a fixed price and by a specified date. The long put can be used as an alternative method for trading on pessimism about price. As the futures price declines, the put's value grows.

The choices for sellers are more limited than those for buyers. When you sell options, you give up the choice of whether or not to exercise. So you might be required to deliver called stock or to have stock put to you if and when a buyer exercises your short option. Figure 8-1 summarizes the benefits and contingent obligations of option trades.

All options are tied to a specific futures contract or range of

FIGURE 8.1. COMPARISONS BETWEEN CALLS AND PUTS

	CALL	PUT
BUYER	has a right but not a requirement to:	
	buy 100 shares at a fixed price	sell 100 shares at a fixed price
SELLER	could be required to:	
	sell 100 shares at a fixed price	buy 100 shares at a fixed price

contracts. The most likely venue for trading in these contracts is going to occur in futures-based indices or ETFs, many of which allow option activity. The option cannot be transferred from one specified underlying security to another. That underlying security, by definition, is a particular futures contract (referring to one commodity and one delivery date), a group of futures (such as energy or agriculture) or a pooled product (an ETF or index fund).

The leveraging aspect of options is what makes them attractive. You can control a number of contracts (or, in the case of ETFs and indices, shares) for each option you buy or sell, and this has a two-part effect many traders find attractive. First, you can use a small amount of capital to create potential profits in a larger base of the futures market; second, you can limit risks, because when you go long in options the maximum you can lose is the amount you pay to buy the option. In comparison, buying or selling contracts directly or going short in any market can involve considerable risk, which is what frightens away so many would-be futures traders. Options present the perfect solution, assuming you master the terminology and trading rules as a first step.

Both calls and puts are defined by a series of terms. The first term is the type of option, call or put. Second, all options refer to specific underlying securities. Next is the strike price, the fixed and unchanging price at which that option can be exercised. The option's value rises or falls based on the proximity between the fixed strike price and the current market value of the futures contract (or fund value). The expiration date is the last of these basic terms. That is the date by which the option has to be exercised or closed. If the open option remains open until after expiration, it immediately becomes worthless.

The strike price of every option is a fixed value for the underlying security. In other words, if a buyer exercises the option (or if its seller experiences exercise) it must occur at the strike price. If the value of the underlying security rises, the value of calls will rise too; and the value of puts will fall. If the value of the underlying security falls, the value of calls will fall too; and the value of puts will rise. Although the increase or decrease in value is based on what would occur if the option were exercised, the majority of options buyers are more likely to sell the appreciated option at a profit. So the profit is made in the net difference between purchase and sell prices. If the trader goes short, the profit occurs in a reverse sequence: sell, hold, and buy. For example, if you open a short option position at 4, you are paid at the time the "sell to open" order is placed. You are paid $400. Later, when the option's value has diminished to $100, for example, you close it out by entering a "buy to close" order. You pay $100 and realize a profit of $300. As a seller, you can also just let the short position expire, and realize the entire $400 as profit. Of course, the risks of going short on options are considerable. So even though the profit potential is considerable for option short sellers, so is the risk.

All options expire in the future. Traditional listed options last only a few months, and Long-Term Equity AnticiPation Securities (LEAPS) options last up to 30 months. However, options on futures contracts are more limited than those on stocks. Shares of stock are going to last for many years, so no stock-based expiration or delivery date is at issue. However, futures contracts all expire within a few months. Thus, options on futures contracts cannot last longer than the contracts themselves.

This leads to an oddity you do not see in stock-based options, where there is only one class of common stock on which options can be written. Options on futures contracts are essentially contracts on contracts. Futures are written on underlying commodities, and options are written on futures contracts. So you may discover that futures indices and ETFs will have a large number of options, all short-term. For example, the GSCI index as of January 2008 has more than 80 current options available, expiring between January and July, or between one week and six months. Even more volume of activity is found in the oil ETF, United States Oil Fund (USO). This ETF offers more than 360 current options, expiring within one week and six months.

There tend to be far fewer stock-based options because with stocks, option strike prices are normally occurring at 5-point intervals. (For lower-priced stocks, $2^1/_2$ point intervals are also available, and for stocks trading above $100 per share, the interval moves up to 10 points.) In comparison, both of the commodity-based options (GSG and USO) trade in 1-point increments. GSG closed on the sample day at $52.65 per share, and options were active with strike prices between $39 and $55. The USO was even more active. On the same day, it closed at $73.09 and options were active between expiration of one week and six months, with strike prices between $40 and $105.

The variety and flexibility of option strikes and expiration dates translates to a larger number of option alternatives and strategies. In addition, the risk level is entirely up to the option trader. Going long—buying calls if you think the share price is going to rise or buying puts if you think it will decline—is a reasonably safe form of speculation. The most you can lose is the premium cost of each option. In comparison, going short, i.e., selling calls if you think the price is going to fall or selling puts if you think the price is going to rise, involves much greater risk. Short sellers can lose a lot of money if the index of ETF goes in the direction opposite of the short seller's estimate. The loss is somewhat mitigated, because short sellers receive the premium when the option is sold. However, exercise can be expensive if the index price moves significantly away from the strike price. For example, if you sold a July 2008 54 call on GSG, you would receive $462 based on the last price. But if the share price rose 10 points above that level by July, the call would be exercised, and you would be required to deliver 100 shares of GSG at $54 per share, even though market value was $64. This loss of $10 per share ($1,000) minus the original call sales price of $462 translates to a net loss of $538 (plus transaction fees on both sides of the trade).

The risk levels of futures on options are significant because traders have to be aware of not only profit potential but also of loss potential. Speculating on futures contracts can be expensive, even through an ETF. However, options enable you to control shares of a tracking index of ETF for a small fraction of the share price. In the previous example, you could trade a single option for under $500 while controlling 100 shares that would cost $5,265 to purchase without the use of options. So the leveraging feature of options is very attractive.

However, before determining whether a particular option is a good bargain or not, you also have to analyze the proximity of strike price to current market value.

Valuation of Options

When you look at option listings, you find a range of current values. Table 8-1 summarizes the closing option listings for a portion of GSG on January 11, 2008.

First, remember that each option controls or relates to 100 shares of stock in the underlying security. In this example, all the April calls and puts are listed. GSG closed on the day at $52.65, and most of the call and put action take place on the 53 contracts. The "53" is the strike price, and the open interest (the number of active contracts) is highest because this is the closest strike price to the current market value of GSG.

The "last" column shows the last price at which each option was traded. In those instances where last is quite different than the bid and ask, it usually means no trades have occurred recently. Check the April 47 call, which had no trading and no open interest, a zero value in the last, and relatively high bid and ask values.

A "bid" is the price at which the option was most recently sold, and an "ask" is the latest price at which it was bought. The difference, called the spread, represents the profit the floor trader, market maker, or specialist earns for executing a trade.

TABLE 8.1. iSHARES S&P GSCI COMMODITY INDEXED OPTION LISTINGS
GSG—$52.65—1/11/08

Calls	Last	Bid	Ask	Volume	Open Interest	Puts	Last	Bid	Ask	Volume	Open Interest
APR46 08	7.50	7.00	7.50	3	1	APR46 08	0	3.50	0.50	0	0
APR47 08	0	6.20	6.70	0	0	APR47 08	1.00	0.45	0.65	0	5
APR48 08	6.20	5.40	5.90	0	38	APR48 08	1.60	0.65	0.85	0	3
APR49 08	5.20	4.70	5.10	0	11	APR49 08	2.40	0.90	1.10	0	4
APR50 08	4.30	4.00	4.40	0	2	APR50 08	1.20	1.20	1.40	0	4
APR53 08	2.60	2.35	2.75	20	122	APR53 08	3.50	2.45	2.80	0	10
APR55 08	2.35	1.60	1.85	0	71	APR55 08	4.40	3.60	4.00	0	1

"Volume" is the number of trades made during the reported session. And "open interest" is the number of active, open option contracts at the end of the day.

By looking over the range of latest prices for each strike price in an option, you can judge relative value. The value is going to vary by two factors. First is proximity between current market value and the option's strike price. For example, the April 53 call is quite close to the current market value of GSG of $52.65; and the April 46 is many points below. The second factor affecting the option's premium value is the time left until expiration. In this case, the April options had three months to go before the April expiration. The April 53 call last traded at 2.60 (this abbreviation translates to $260). But if you check the January 53 call, set to expire in only one week from the January 11 date, it was trading at only 0.40 ($40).

This difference consists of time value, or the degree of an option's premium that can be assigned to the time remaining until expiration. If it were possible to isolate time value alone, you would see it decline at an accelerating rate as the expiration date approaches. Figure 8-2 summarizes this trend in time value.

As you might expect, time value is only part of the overall premium value in an option. There is also intrinsic value. This is the portion of a call when current market value of the underlying security is higher than the strike price, or the portion of a put when current market value of the underlying security is lower than the strike price. For example, GSG's current market value in the example was $52.65. The April 53 call contained no intrinsic value, but the April 50 was reported at 4.30 ($430). Of this, 2.65 points were intrinsic value and the remaining 1.65 points were time value:

Intrinsic value	**$265**
Time value	**165**
Total premium	**$430**

All the calls shown above the current market value had no intrinsic value, and their entire premium consisted of time value. The put is opposite. So when a put's value is higher than current market value, it contains some intrinsic value. The 50 put has no intrinsic

FIGURE 8.2. TIME VALUE PREMIUM

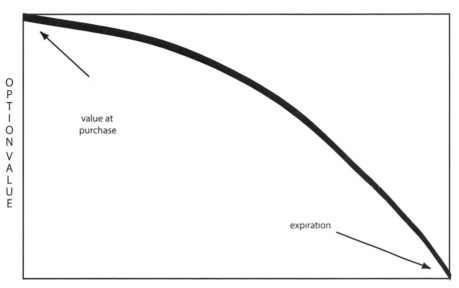

O
P
T
I
O
N

V
A
L
U
E

value at
purchase

expiration

T I M E

value, but the April 53 put (worth 3.50, or $350) was 0.35 above
current market value of GSG, so its intrinsic value was $35:

Intrinsic value	$ 35
Time value	315
Total premium	**$350**

The distinction of a call's being above or below the strike price
is defined as being "in the money" (current market value of the
underlying security is higher than a call's strike or lower than a
put's strike); out of the money (current market value of the underlying security is lower than a call strike or higher than a put strike);
or at the money, which occurs when the current market value of
the underlying security is exactly the same as the strike price of the
option.

Figure 8-3 summarizes the comparative relationship of the underlying security to call or put strike prices.

The option premium contains a combination of intrinsic and
time value, and no intrinsic value exists when at the money or out
of the money. However, time value premium often acts in a volatile

FIGURE 8.3. INTRINSIC VALUE

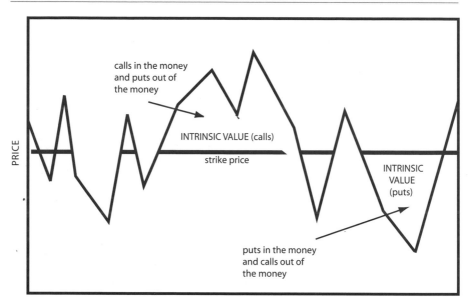

manner, rising or falling to a higher or lower degree than you would expect in a predictable world. This aspect of option valuation, usually lumped in as a part of time value, is actually quite distinct. It could be called "volatility premium," because it varies based on interest in both the underlying security and the option contract itself. It is also called extrinsic value. This is the portion of premium that makes any option trading uncertain, because it cannot be predicted. If you isolate pure time value, the course of erosion is fairly predictable based on time, and the rate of acceleration is also predictable. Intrinsic value is also quite simple to compute. Each dollar of in the money in the underlying security translates to one dollar of intrinsic premium value in the option. To the extent that option premium values vary from these predictable models, it represents the volatility of the contract and underlying security.

Strategy Basics: An Overview

Finding the best option trading strategy involves testing your own assumptions and risk tolerance levels. If you are going to trade options on futures, either directly or through a pooled index or

ETF, you first need to make sure that the decision is a good match for you. A five-part analysis helps make this decision.

1. *Master terminology and trading rules.* The most difficult part of options is learning the language, which involves a lot of jargon. Each definition contains important distinguishing features of option trading and the risks involved; in addition, you need to get approved by your brokerage firm to even trade options. As part of the approval process, your broker assigns a trading level based on your knowledge and experience as well as the dollar size of your account. Getting through this first step can be daunting, because it appears complex at first. However, once you get over the initial hurdle, you will find options to be an excellent addition to a range of strategies within your portfolio.

2. *Identify risk tolerance limits.* Next, you need to understand exactly what kinds of risks you can afford to take and are willing to take. Not everyone can tolerate the same level of risk. This decision is based on income, size of your portfolio, and experience as a trader and investor. You need to carefully and completely define your risk tolerance level before making any decisions.

3. *Match risk tolerance to strategies.* There are many possible option strategies to choose from. The mere decision of using futures-based pools as a vehicle for options is itself the result of analyzing your risk tolerance level and concluding that these options are a sound way to proceed. Some strategies are conservative, others very high risk. So you need to ensure that you are in control of risk by the kinds of option-based strategies you decide to pursue.

4. *Identify your trading goal.* Some traders use options to insure long positions. This hedge involves holding long puts so that, in the event the underlying security loses value, that loss will be offset by higher value in the puts. Others use options to swing trade, buying calls or selling puts at price dips, and doing the opposite when prices climb to high levels. In between these examples of the strategic uses of options there is a range of many other possibilities.

5. *Find a good match between strategy, risk, and goal.* The ultimate purpose in analyzing options is to decide whether you will be able to find a strategy that is also a solid match for your own risk toler-

ance, and that will help you achieve your goal. That goal can be short-term cash profits, insurance, hedging, or pure speculation. As long as you know in advance what you want to achieve, you have a good chance of finding the best strategy, or deciding that options are *not* a good fit for you.

There are a few basic strategies everyone should know. Beginning with long positions, remember that as the owner of an option, you are never required to exercise. You can exercise if you want, sell at any time, or allow the option to expire worthless. In the long position, you have all the control and you decide when and if to make a decision.

Buying calls is the most popular basic option strategy. Calls are more popular than puts because most people think that commodity prices are going to rise. Buying puts only works if prices fall, so puts are more easily overlooked. But even call buyers face a difficult task in trying to profit consistently from speculating in options. About three-quarters of all options expire worthless, meaning there is only a one-in-four chance that you will make a profit from buying calls. Even so, most speculators believe they can beat the odds.

For example, Table 8-2 summarizes five listings for the U.S. Oil Fund as of the close of business on January 11, 2008.

The day's close for USO was $73.09, so the 73 calls and those above that level were slightly out of the money; and those calls higher than that level were also out of the money. Thus, they represent a range of calls of substantial interest to option traders. In addition, there were six months to go until expiration, which is an attractive range. Given that USO closed at $73.09, the July 73 calls were attractive, especially to those believing that the price of oil was going to rise.

Buying puts works in reverse. The put increases in value when the market value of the underlying security falls. The more it falls, the more valuable the put becomes. So if you believe a commodity is overpriced and that it will retreat in the near future, long puts may be the way to go. For example, referring back to Table 8-2, all the listed puts were in the money. (Remember, puts work in reverse order from calls, so when the put strikes are higher than current market value, they are in the money.) In this situation, the July 73

TABLE 8.2. UNITED STATES OIL FUND OPTIONS LISTINGS
USO—$73.09—1/11/08

Calls	Last	Bid	Ask	Volume	Open Interest	Puts	Last	Bid	Ask	Volume	Open Interest
JUL73 08	6.60	6.20	6.60	11	137	JUL73 08	6.30	5.20	6.60	0	160
JUL74 08	7.93	5.70	6.20	0	81	JUL74 08	5.80	5.70	7.10	0	141
JUL75 08	5.50	5.30	5.70	4	120	JUL75 08	7.60	7.30	7.70	16	294
JUL76 08	6.10	5.00	5.40	0	113	JUL76 08	6.60	7.90	8.30	0	143
JUL77 08	5.10	4.60	5.00	2	83	JUL77 08	6.80	8.50	9.00	0	120

put is only slightly in the money. So if you believed that oil prices were going to fall in the coming six months, this would have been a play worth considering. Because the July 73 put is in the money, intrinsic value will increase point for point with a decline in USO (although that may also be offset by declining time value during the same period).

Buyers of options face a problem in picking the right option, whether calls or puts. No matter which option you select, the longer the time until expiration, the higher the cost is going to be. It is desirable to have more time rather than less, because you need time for the underlying security to rise enough to produce a profit. Additionally, the most promising options are those close to the strike price; but these will be more expensive than those further out of the money. If you look only for bargain-priced options, you have a smaller chance of making a profit.

The option has to increase enough in value to cover your initial cost *and* to grow in intrinsic value before expiration. So if you pay 5 ($500) for a call that will expire in six months and it is at the money, you will need that commodity to rise five points just to break even. That has to occur before expiration. If you pay 4 ($400) for a put that is at the money and has four months to go until expiration, you will need the commodity to fall four points just to break even, and that has to happen within the next four months.

The basic long strategies for option trading are not high risk. The most you can lose is the price you pay for the option. In comparison, the short side of option trades may contain much greater risks. So even though potential losses are limited in long positions, remember that there is only about a one-in-four chance that you will make a profit.

Traders use long calls and puts for many reasons. Some are just speculating in the short-term roller coaster of play variance, while others are attempting to take advantage of short-term price dips, protect paper profits, or take profits without selling commodities through small but consistent option profits.

Advanced Strategies

The speculative long call and put is perhaps the most popular option strategy. It is simple, losses are limited, and traders enjoy telling their friends how they doubled their money in only three days. (Of course, they forget to also mention that that happened only once in four attempts.)

Another variation of option strategies is the short position. In the futures market, you will probably want to avoid shorting the futures contract directly because it could involve significant risks. However, with the use of options, those risks can be reduced. You can write short calls in one of two ways. First is the naked short call. This occurs when you do not own shares of the underlying security. Believing that the price of USO is going to fall, for example, you may decide to sell a July 74 call. Referring back to Table 8-2, note that this call was exceptionally rich (meaning higher than surrounding options), closing at 7.93 ($793). This is somewhat misleading, however. Note that the bid/ask spread was 5.70 to 6.20, much lower; and that no trading occurred on that day. So if you were to sell this call, you would probably receive a much lower premium. This short call remains attractive, however, if you are willing to take the naked call risk.

When you sell an option, the premium amount is placed into your account when the trade is complete. Your brokerage firm will impose margin requirements when you sell naked options, and you also have to be qualified to trade at an acceptable position to be allowed to write naked options. As long as the underlying security's market value falls, you will make a profit. If the option expires out of the money, you keep the entire amount; or you can enter a "buy to close" order once the call's value has declined, pay the current value and book a profit on the position.

The risk is that the short call could be exercised. This can occur at any time before expiration when the call is in the money, although it is most likely right before expiration. In the event of exercise, you would be required to purchase 100 shares of USO at current market value, and then deliver it at the strike value. For example, if you sold a July 74 call and it was exercised (called) at a point when USO had gone to $80 per share, you would lose $600. Your actual loss would be reduced by the amount of call premium received at the time you opened the short call. For example, if you received 5, your net loss on this trade would be $300 (eight points for the difference between market value and strike, less five points you were paid when you sold the call).

The risk of the naked, or uncovered, call is too great for most traders. In comparison, you can also sell a *covered call*, which is probably the most conservative strategy possible. In this case, you own 100 shares of the underlying security for each call you sell. In this example, you might have bought 100 shares of USO at $68 per share. If you sell a covered call for July at strike of 74, you would profit in two ways. First, you keep the call premium you are paid; second, you earn a capital gain on the investment of $600 (strike of $74 per share minus your basis of $68).

You can also sell puts, although it is not possible to create a "covered" put in the same way you can create a covered call. However, the risks of a short put are far less than those for an uncovered call. While the underlying security's market value can rise indefinitely, at least in theory, it can only fall so far. In the worst case, it could fall to zero, but that would mean the components of the pool would also have to lose all value. That is not likely to happen in any scenario. For example, if you were to write a put on USO, you can estimate the maximum risk by calculating the potential lowest point to which the component futures contracts could fall. So if oil was at about $98 per barrel in the beginning of January 2008, what were the odds of the price falling within six months to $90, $80, or $70?

The point is that putting aside the theory for the moment, the realistic range of likely market risk is quite small in writing puts against pooled futures indices or ETFs. You benefit from the diversified portfolio as well as from the realistic range of likely price movements in the futures contracts.

For example, if you had sold a July 73 put in the beginning of January 2008, the premium somewhere between $620 and $660 would be placed in your account. If you believe oil prices were likely to rise, this would be a worthwhile form of speculation. USO closed at $73.09; so as long as prices remained above $73, exercise would not occur. If the USO market value fell even six points, your put premium income would create a small profit or break even. If the USO market value fell lower than $67 per share, you would lose.

Short option positions can be rolled forward in the same way that futures contract holdings are rolled forward. When expiration nears, short option positions in the money can be closed and replaced with later-expiring contracts. This can be accomplished at the same strike or a different one. For example, let's say you had sold a naked call expiring in January 2008 at 70. Just before expiration, on January 11, that contract closed at 3.20 ($320). If you took no action, it would be exercised, since USO was at $73.09 per share; the option was three points in the money. To avoid exercise, you could "buy to close" the January 70 and replace it. You have several choices. The February 70 call closed at 4.50, so you could roll into that position and realize $130 profit (minus transaction fees). This not only creates additional profit; it also avoids or delays likely exercise. But it leaves your open position in the money. You could also replace the January call with an April 74, which closed at 4.30 ($430). This yields $110 and leaves you in a short position for three more months. However, it replaces the about-to-expire short call with another call out of the money.

Since in-the-money puts move in the opposite position, you would want to roll a short in-the-money put forward to avoid exercise, or forward and down to a new strike. For example, if you had sold a January 75, you would face imminent exercise. So to avoid this, you could buy to close the January 75 put (which closed at 2.55) and replace it with a February 75 put (which closed at 4.10), and realize a profit of $155 while also putting off the likely exercise. (Remember, in-the-money options can be exercised at any time, but the most likely timing is right before expiration.) Another alternative would be to replace the January 75 and replace it with an April 72 put. That closed at 4.10, so you would realize the same profit as with a February 75 replacement. However, you commit yourself to three more months while lowering the likely strike price and taking the short position out of the money.

Rolling grants you substantial flexibility to avoid exercise of short positions. In both USO and GSG, for example, option contracts occur in one-dollar increments. At the same price levels for stocks, options would only be available in five-point increments. In many instances, this gap makes it more difficult to produce net credit in rolling without going out more months, or without being able to pick the strike level you desire.

You can roll both naked and covered calls to avoid exercise, as well as short puts. As long as you avoid exercise and produce additional profits, rolling is effective as a means for also adding future profits to your position. Even if eventually exercised, the rolled option will produce higher capital gains. For example, if you replace a current 70 call with a later-expiring 74 call, if and when that is exercised, you earn $400 more in capital gains. And if you roll a put down from 75 to 72, upon exercise you gain an additional $300 capital gain, or reduce a capital loss by $300. For many option traders, exercise will be a rare event. By remaining diligent in tracking short positions to avoid exercise, you will be able to avoid going in the money on a majority of open short positions, continually rolling forward and up (for short calls) or forward and down (for short puts).

■ Combining Options

So far, the strategies explained have been limited to the use of single options. You can go long a call or a put, or go short a call or a put. Using multiple contracts increases both risk exposure and potential profit. When writing covered calls, owning multiple increments of 100 shares of an underlying security also increases the potential strategies. For example, you can write a range of different covered calls involving various strikes and expirations. You can also use ratio writes, which mitigate risks of uncovered call writing while augmenting income. For example, if you own 400 shares and write five calls, you have a five-to-four ratio write.

There is more to the possible strategic uses of options for futures investing. The use of options becomes truly interesting when you move into the more advanced realm of spreads and straddles.

A *spread* is a strategy in which you buy and sell options on the same underlying security at the same time, but with different expiration, strike, or both. You can accomplish a spread by buying or selling, and using either calls or puts. For example, a *bull call spread* is designed to produce profits when the underlying security rises in value. You buy a call at one strike and sell a call at another, higher strike. For example, referring to Table 8-2, you may buy a USO July 75 call and sell a July 76. The net difference between these two is only $60, so you receive that amount for opening the spread. If the USO market value remains below $75 per share, the position would expire worthless and you keep the $60 difference. If the market value rose above the $76-per-share level, the short call could be exercised, but the long position would protect all but $100 of that position. In that outcome, you could roll the short 76 call forward to avoid exercise and sell the 75, either at a profit or (if time value evaporated) at a loss. The risk in the long bull spread is minimal, but so is the potential profit.

A *bear spread* involves the same basic approach, but using long puts. For example, in the case of USO, you could have bought a July 74, which closed at 5.80 on January 11; and sold a July 73, which closed at 6.30. Your net income in this situation would have been $50. If the value of USO were to rise, you get to keep the $50 as net profit. However, if it fell below the $73-per-share level, the short 73 would risk exercise, while the long 74 could be closed. The short put could be rolled forward and down to avoid exercise. Like the long bull spread, the long bear spread offers limited risk along with limited profit.

It is also possible to create a bull spread employing puts, or a bear spread with calls. The position of strike prices is simply reversed. Spreads are many and varied, and many also involve varying the expiration date, or both expiration and strike.

A *straddle* is a different strategy altogether, in which you open both a call and a put at the same strike price and expiration. You can open a straddle on either the long or the short side. An example of a long straddle on GSG (see Table 8-1) would involve opening two April 53 positions. The 53 call closed at 2.60 and the put closed at 3.50. So the cost of opening a long straddle would be $610. The value of GSG at this point was $52.65 per share. So given the fact that this straddle cost $610 to open, if the stock were to move down to $46.55 or up to $58.75—a total range of 12.20 points—this straddle would not be profitable. You would need a larger move than this "loss zone" move to produce a profit. A long straddle is appropriate when you expect a big move but you're not sure of the direction it will take.

A short straddle involves selling both a call and a put of the same expiration and strike. For example on GSG, you could sell an

April 53 call for 2.60 and an April 53 put for 3.50, in which case you *receive* $610. Because you receive rather than pay, the previously indicated price range between $46.55 and $58.75 becomes a "profit zone" rather than a loss zone. As long as GSG remains in this price range between January and the April expiration, the short straddle would be profitable. Even if one side or the other were exercised, the option premium offsets the cost. (This calculation does not include transaction fees; however, those should be minimal if you use an online discount brokerage service.)

The short straddle involves considerable risks if the underlying security is volatile. However, this risk can be minimized if you also own 100 shares of the underlying security, GSG in this case. Then the straddle becomes a combination of a covered call and an uncovered put. You start out with a $610 profit even if one side or the other is exercised. If the call is exercised, your 100 shares of GSG would be called away; and as long as your original cost was lower than $53 per share, that would produce a capital gain. If the put is exercised, you would have another 100 shares put to you at $53 per share, even though the price of GSG would be lower. So as long as you consider $53 per share a good price, exercise of the put would not be bad news. A few additional points to keep in mind:

1. *Either side can be rolled to avoid exercise, producing additional income.* You can roll either the call or the put to avoid exercise. In volatile situations, you can also roll both, widening the gap between current market value and eventual exercise price. It is conceivable that you may avoid exercise indefinitely in this strategy.

2. *Exercise of the short put could lead to an additional profitable short straddle with 200 shares.* If and when the put is exercised, it doubles your position in the underlying security. Assuming you want 200 shares rather than 100, this enables you to create additional option income by writing a new short straddle. Now you can write two calls and two puts. The two calls would be covered and the two puts would be naked. Assuming you still like the price per share of the underlying security, this is one way to recover the short option loss.

3. *Exercise of the put could produce a net loss, which could be offset by writing subsequent covered calls.* The net basis in the underlying security upon exercise would be the average of the original basis plus the exercised basis of the additional 100 shares. As long as calls are available with strike prices greater than the average basis in the underlying security, you can create additional covered call profits without writing a new short straddle. These new covered calls can later be rolled forward again to avoid exercise.

The use of options on futures indices and ETFs vastly expands your potential strategic approaches to this market. The futures market appears cumbersome and involves many steps just to place orders; a solution is to enter this market through pooled venues such as futures indices and ETFs. You really expand your potential strategies by picking ones allowing you to buy and sell options. Because these listed indices and ETFs trade just like stocks, but use one-point strike increments, they are extremely flexible.

Option trading provides the best of both worlds: Access to fast-moving futures contracts, without the risk and high cost of trading futures positions directly.

This concludes Part 2. Part 3 describes in detail each of the major futures markets, one chapter for each sector.

CLASSIFICATIONS OF FUTURES

				5 Yr. Treasury Not
			June	111-087 111
			Sept	110-285 110
		19.962	2 Yr. Treasury Note
		98.525	June	106-007 106-
			30 Day Federal Fund.
		15.673	April	97.735 97.7
		140.673	May	97.930 97.96
		91.584		
		66.543	1 Month Libor (CME)-$
		55.727	May	97.2100 97.240
		43.819	June	97.2850 97.2950
			Eurodollar (CME)-$1,000.0
			May	97.1450 97.1925
			June	97.1200 97.2150
22.75	104,553		Sept	97.0400 97.1500
22.75	567,041		Dec	96.8600 96.9700
03	191		**Currency Futures**	

THE ENERGY MARKET

This chapter provides an overview of the energy market, demand trends, and a range of futures contracts (Brent crude oil, light crude, heating oil, natural gas, propane, and ethanol). Included are market explanations of the primary oil market as well as secondary and alternative energy markets.

Energy is the largest of all futures markets, and growing. More futures trading occurs in the major oil-related futures than in any other. Energy prices affect all segments of society, and thus energy is a core economic force. It is also a political force, and as conflict or tensions arise in oil-producing nations, prices rise around the world. Energy prices affect agricultural prices directly as transportation and production costs rise, so it is unlikely that the cycles in the energy market will be downward in a big way at any time in the near future.

Basics of Energy Markets

Beyond the broad economic trends you can find with market-wide sources, you also will be able to locate useful information focused on specific futures. The energy market, for example, affects virtually every other futures market. Because any shipment from production to store requires truck, rail, air, and sea transportation, energy prices have risen in recent years to record-level highs. The cost of keeping businesses open, heated, and lit all require energy; all manufacturing and production efforts also demand energy use, and the more intense the activity, the more energy it requires.

Crude oil experiences more trading volume than any other contracts, and it is used for 40% of worldwide energy consumption. Most economists agree that oil is the most important link in Western countries, and the lack of oil would cause recessions, as was the case following the oil embargo by OPEC in 1973. Given the indispensable nature of oil in so many aspects of the economy, it is clear why energy futures are so popular, and why they represent a promising commodity to trade. Even if you determine that alternative fuel sources are going to benefit from increasing prices, commodities such as ethanol and corn are affected directly as well.

The United States imports more oil from Canada than from anywhere else. As Figure 9-1 shows, the level of imports (based on the number of barrels per day at the end of 2007) does not rely on the Middle East as much as many people believe. In fact, 35% of all imports come from Canada and Mexico.

Production in Canada is likely to rise in the near future. According to data published by the Canadian Association of Petroleum Producers (CAPP, www.capp.ca), oil sands contain massive reserves, estimated at 175 billion barrels. As of the end of 2006, oil sand production represented 39% of Canada's total oil production, or 1 million barrels per day. CAPP estimates that by 2020, that will grow to 4 million barrels per day. The United States could extract a considerable number of reserves in the Arctic National Wildlife Refuge (ANWR). Although controversial, this area in northern Alaska may hold up to one-half of the total U.S. oil reserves. According to one study:

> ANWR, located in the northeast corner of Alaska entirely above the Arctic Circle, comprises 19.6 million acres of the Brooks Range of mountains and Arctic Coastal Plain abutting the Canadian Border

*FIGURE 9.1. PETROLEUM IMPORTS BY COUNTRY, 2007 (BARRELS PER DAY,
IN THOUSANDS)*

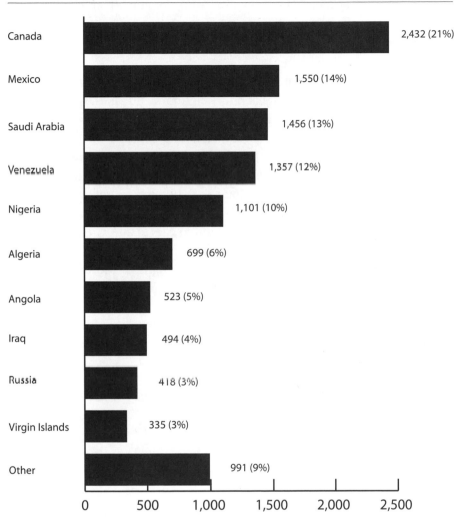

Canada — 2,432 (21%)
Mexico — 1,550 (14%)
Saudi Arabia — 1,456 (13%)
Venezuela — 1,357 (12%)
Nigeria — 1,101 (10%)
Algeria — 699 (6%)
Angola — 523 (5%)
Iraq — 494 (4%)
Russia — 418 (3%)
Virgin Islands — 335 (3%)
Other — 991 (9%)

0   500   1,000   1,500   2,000   2,500

Source: www.eia.doe.gov, accessed December 28, 2007.

and the Arctic Ocean. According to the U.S. Geological Survey, the
Coastal Plain of ANWR could contain up to 16 billion barrels of recoverable oil.

That would make it the largest single oil reserve in North
America, containing almost *half* of the total U.S. known reserves of

oil. ANWR could, the Energy Information Administration reports, yield more than 1 million barrels of oil a day for more than thirty years. This is enough oil to replace *approximately 30 years of oil imports from Saudi Arabia.*[1]

Although the United States imports most of its oil (about 65%), most of that comes from friendly neighbors and allies. And contrary to many claims that the U.S. involvement in Iraq was devised to get that country's oil, only a very small percentage of imported oil comes from that country. Production levels may be more important for futures prices than proven reserves, but all oil-producing countries have incentive to continue producing and selling oil to the major consumers. Over 85 million barrels per day are used up, and the two largest oil users are the United States and China.

Crude oil prices have risen dramatically over the past few years. Between 1999 and 2007, the price of light crude oil rose from about $14 per barrel up to nearly $100. Figure 9-2 summarizes this nine-year trend.

Investing in the oil industry can be accomplished through individual company stocks, ETFs, or commodity indices. Major oil companies include:

Company	Market Symbol	Cap 12/07
ExxonMobil	XOM	$503B
PetroChina	PTR	315
PetroleoBrasileiro	PBR	241
BP	BP	235
Chevron	CVX	197

Energy-based ETFs include the following, all trading on the AMEX:

U.S. Oil Fund (USO)

PowerShares DB Oil Fund (DBO)

iShares S&P Global Energy Sector (IXC)

Energy Select Sector SPDR (XLE)

iShares Goldman Sachs Natural Resources (IGE)

FIGURE 9.2. LIGHT CRUDE OIL, PRICE PER BARREL, 1999–2007

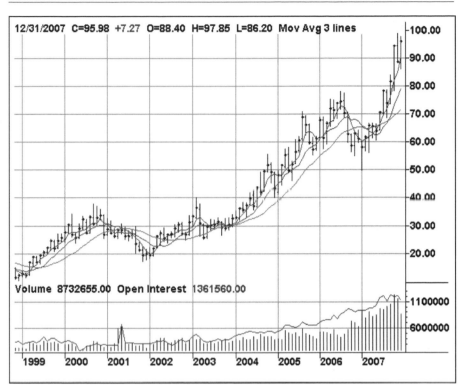

Source: Charts provided courtesy of TradingCharts.com: http//futures.tradingcharts.com; created with SuperCharts by Omega Research © 1997.

Energy indices include:

Name	Percent in energy
GSCI	73.0%
S&P Commodity Index	53.0
RICI	44.0
Reuters/Jeffries CRB	17.6

You can also trade commodities through a broker, in the following categories:

Commodity Name and Type	Exchange
Brent Crude Oil	IPE (International Petroleum Exchange)
Ethanol	CBOT

Light Crude Oil	NYMEX
NYH RBOB Gasoline	NYMEX
Gas-Oil	IPE
Heating Oil	NYMEX
Natural Gas	NYMEX
Propane	NYMEX
Unleaded Gas	NYMEX

The importance and dominance of energy commodities trading—as both a necessity and as a defining economic force—is obvious based on rising prices per barrel, scarcity of domestic supply versus demand, and anticipated higher demand in the future. This all makes energy futures a promising futures trade. In trading futures, two dominant factors should be kept in mind: supplies on hand in refineries and production capacity. Accidents or weather-related causes of shutdowns directly affect petroleum prices in the short term (Hurricane Katrina, for example, after which 16 refineries were shut down, many for more than a full year).

Crude oil is the most followed energy commodity, but other important futures trades can also be made in unleaded gasoline, heating oil, and ethanol. In addition to the obvious domestic supply and demand and refinery capacity as price factors, the geopolitical climate also affects oil prices. When Bhutto was assassinated in December 2007, oil prices approached $100, even though Pakistan does not export oil. The regional tension, however, did have a direct effect. Political tension impacts oil even more than the often-cited "safe haven" of gold. Anticipation of future prices has as much to do with prices as OPEC policies or world tensions, and speculation in energy futures only increases whenever the markets worry about future supplies and prices.

The Basics of Fossil Fuels

Because crude oil is a limited resource, it will eventually run out. Although today's reserves seem high, usage has been rising in past decades so at some point the demand for crude oil will outpace the actual reserves. By that time, the world will need to have found alternate sources of energy, or discovered ways to use oil more efficiently. Oil itself exists in the ground, under the ocean, and in sand deposits. Also known as "fossil fuel," oil is believed to have been formed over millions of years from the remains of long-dead plants and animals. The organic layers that formed and were covered by sand over many millions of years eventually formed into crude oil and natural gas. So in a sense, oil is a recycled product of organic material. Crude oil consists of hydrocarbons, or molecular remains of hydrogen and carbon atoms.

Various products are derived from distillation of crude oil. Each chemical compound within oil has a separate boiling point. Crude oil is distilled by burning off each product at its specific boiling point. Figure 9-3 shows this process.

So crude oil is heated in a still column so that lighter products—for example, liquid petroleum gas (LPG), naphtha, and straight-run gasoline—can be recovered at various temperatures. Middle-level products come next, including jet fuel, kerosene, home heating oil, and diesel fuel. Last, the heavy products are distilled, including residuum and residual fuel oils.

FIGURE 9.3. CRUDE OIL DISTILLATION: THE FIRST STEP

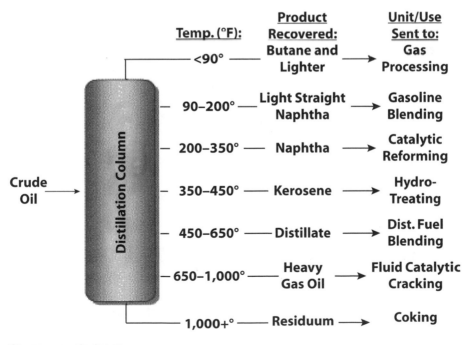

Source: www.eia.doe.gov.

Oil is "mined" in various ways. Most people are familiar with the most common, land-based or sea-based drilling. Rigs are constructed on the ground or on sea platforms, based on the location of three key attributes. First the area must contain source rock that indicates crude oil probably has formed. Second, that rock needs to be richly populated with organic material that has been converted to oil. Third, the oil must have migrated to an accumulation area called reservoir rock. This is normally sandstone or limestone, porous enough to hold oil reserves. Assuming there is an adequate reserve of such oil on hand to justify the cost of exploration and drilling, the extraction process begins.

This requires introducing pressure adequate to force oil to the surface. This includes a combination of natural pressure built up within the reservoir, which, when released, brings oil upward, and additional pumping to bring up additional supplies. This continues as long as production is high enough to cover costs and produce profits. But once an oil well ceases to produce oil profitably, it is capped and abandoned. It is interesting that as oil prices rise, some abandoned oil wells become viable once again. If oil profits can be achieved from once-abandoned wells, this secondary source can produce additional recoverable reserves. Only a few decades ago, domestic oil reserves were viewed as quite limited, because the cost-benefit ratio simply wasn't good enough. But with higher oil prices, recoverable reserves have grown.

A relatively new, advanced method for crude oil extraction is horizontal drilling. Under this method, a vertical drill begins the process, but it is then moved in an arc so that additional reserves are tapped via horizontal paths. This exposes additional reservoir rock and often expands the potential recoverability of a single well or field. The horizontal drilling method is most effective when working in fractured conventional reserves or source rock as well as to secondary efforts in previously abandoned wells.

Shale Oil and Sand Oil

A promising development beyond traditional drilling is found in shale oil reserves. While extraction is more expensive than from conventional drilling, reserves are enormous. The U.S.-based oil shale deposits are the largest in the world, located primarily in two sites: the Devonian-Mississippian shale in the Appalachian basin and the Green River formation in Colorado, Utah, and Wyoming. These reserves are enormous, estimated between 1.5 and 2.6 *trillion* barrels.[2]

Other worldwide shale reserves are substantial as well. Table 9-1 summarizes the known reserves as of the end of 2005.

Shale is rock-like and rich in kerogen, an organic material. Oil is extracted in two methods. First, the shale is mined and processed through heat and enrichment with hydrogen vaporization. The second involves heating shale while still in the ground until it fractures. This releases gases and liquids, which are then mined. Mining methods yield different levels of oil, since the levels of kerogen content differ as well among fields.

Oil sand deposits are also massive, and extraction methods be-

TABLE 9.1. IN-PLACE SHALE OIL RESERVES, WORLDWIDE

Deposit	Country	Millions of Barrels	Millions of Tonnes
Green River Formation	U.S.	1,466,000	213,000
Phosphoria Formation	U.S.	250,000	35,775
Eastern Devoniam	U.S.	189,000	27,000
Heath Formation	U.S.	180,000	25,578
Olenyok Basin	Russia	167,715	24,000
Congo	Democratic Republic of Congo	100,000	14,310
Irati Formation	Brazil	80,000	11,448
Sicily	Italy	63,000	9,015
Tarfaya	Morocco	42,145	6,448
Volga Basin	Russia	31,447	4,500
St. Petersburg, Baltic Oil Shale Basin	Russia	25,157	3,600
Vychogodsk Basin	Russia	19,580	2,800
Wadi Maghar	Jordan	14,009	2,149
Dictyonema Shale	Estonia	12,386	1,900
Timahdit	Morocco1	1,236	1,719
Collingwood Shale	Canada	12,300	1,717
Italy	Italy	10,000	1,431

Source: World Energy Council (WEC), *Survey of Energy Resources*, 2007, table as of the end of 2005.

come more cost-effective over time. Most oil sand deposits are located in Venezuela and Canada. These deposits have been assigned several names, including tar sands, bituminous sands, and extra-heavy oil. Canada supplies the United States with over 1 million barrels of oil per day, mined from tar sands. In the United States, the Utah tar sand area contains eight major deposits (the largest is the Tar Sand Triangle) with estimated reserves of 32 billion barrels.

It is complicated to mine sand oil because it is mixed with sand as well as water and clay, and has to be removed from its surroundings before it can be refined. This kind of crude oil is called bitumen, and two methods are commonly used in extraction. First is an on-site technique using hot water; about one-fifth of oil sand extraction occurs using this method. Second is a technique applied when oil sands are too far beneath the surface to use the hot water technique. This method employs drilling down and then interjecting steam to reduce the viscosity of the bitumen. The bitumen is then pumped to the surface via wells, and the sand is left behind.

Crude Oil Production

In evaluating sources for "big oil," two major groups have to be distinguished. First is the Organization of Petroleum Exporting Countries (OPEC), founded in 1960 and consisting of 13 nations: five founding members (Saudi Arabia, Iran, Iraq, Kuwait, and Venezuela) and eight additional current members (Qatar, Indonesia, Libya, United Arab Emirates, Algeria, Nigeria, Gabon, and Angola). OPEC member nations depend on oil exports as their primary or sole means of national support and work together to control production levels and prices. The official site of OPEC (www.opec.org) describes its purpose as coordination among its members to ensure a reasonable rate of return on their investment, and to ensure that consuming countries have a stable supply of oil. While this is controversial and many disagree, one of the important factors in supporting oil prices is agreed-upon production levels for each member country, as a contributor to world oil supplies.

Non-OPEC production of crude oil is substantial. The former Soviet Republic collectively is the largest non-OPEC oil producer. In 2005, OPEC produced 42% of all world oil consumed. Of non-

OPEC production, the former Soviet Union (FSU) nations accounted for one-fourth of the total. While OPEC oil production dominated until the mid-1970s, political unrest and rising oil prices led to non-OPEC oil production growth; since that time, non-OPEC nations have produced most world oil. By 2005, these countries were producing nearly 50 million barrels per day, versus OPEC production under 35 million barrels per day.

Government control of much of the production activity in OPEC countries determines not only production levels but cost. In those countries, government-run production dominates private company efforts. For example, in Saudi Arabia, the Saudi family-owned company, Aramco Oil, produces three times more oil than Shell Oil; and oil reserves are approximately seven times higher than Shell, Exxon, BP, and Chevron combined. So the government-run operation has far more influence on oil production and prices, even though non-OPEC production is greater on a worldwide basis. The majority of non-OPEC producers are also net importers of oil, so reliance on world supplies *including* OPEC production gives the OPEC cartel a lot of oil price influence and, as a result, affects oil futures as well.

A long-standing question of when world oil reserves will run out also creates a permanent concern about oil prices. Estimates are continually updated, and, even today with dire predictions of global warming and expended oil supplies, the numbers are simply not known by anyone with certainty. Not only have experts warned that the world is running out of oil (and has been for the past 100 years), but "peak production"—that point where production is at its height and the trend begins to turn downward—has also been continually updated. As new data revise the previous estimate, the forecast is continually moved forward a few years. The following is a brief history of predictions about oil reserves and peak production:

1914—Worldwide oil will last only one decade. (U.S. Bureau of Mines)

1920—worldwide oil supplies total only 20 billion barrels. (U.S. Geological Survey)

1922—The United States has only enough oil supply to last 20 years. (U.S. Geological Survey)

1926—The world supply of oil totals only 4.5 billion barrels. (U.S. Federal Oil Conservation Board)

1932—Only 10 billion barrels of oil remain. (U.S. Federal Oil Conservation Board)

1944—Only 20 billion barrels of oil remain in the worldwide supply. (U.S. Petroleum Administrator for War)

1950—World oil reserves are down to 100 billion barrels. (American Petroleum Institute)

1951—World oil supplies will last only another 13 years. (U.S. Department of the Interior)

1972—Peak production will have been reached by the year 2000. (Report to the UN Conference on Human Environment)

1976—Oil supplies will peak at about the year 2000. (U.K. Department of Energy)

1977—Consumption "could use up all of the proven reserves of oil in the entire world by the end of the next decade." (President Jimmy Carter)

1977—The oil peak will occur in 1996. (Dr. M. King Hubbert)

1979—The plateau of oil production will be reached "within the next 25 years." (expert at Shell Oil)

1981—Oil will "plateau around the turn of the century." (The World Bank)

1995—The peak year will occur in 2005. (Petroconsultants C. J. Campbell and J. H. Laherrère, *The World's Supply of Oil, 1930–2050*)

1997—The peak will occur in 2010 (L. F. Ivanhoe, "Updated Hubbert Curves Analyze World Oil Supply," *World Oil* 217, No. 11 [November 1996]: 91–94) or 2020 (J. D. Edwards, "Crude Oil and Alternative Energy Production Forecasts of the Twenty-First Century: The End of the Hydrocarbon Era," *AAPG Bulletin* 81 [1997]: 1292–1305)

1998—Oil will peak in 2014. (International Energy Agency)

1999—The USGS revised prediction, as well as author C. J. Campbell, chose 2010 as the peak year for oil. (U.S. Geological Survey and author C. J. Campbell, "Oil Reserves and Depletion," *PESGB Newsletter*, Petroleum Exploration Society of Great Britain, (March 1999): pp. 87–90.)

2001—Peak production will occur in 2003. (K. S. Deffeyes, *Hubbert's Peak* Princeton University Press, 2001.)

Hubbert's Peak Theory

To appreciate how supply and demand trends work, you need to first know the nature of the commodity involved. Agricultural commodities are renewable as long as farmers are able to plant and harvest new crops each year; the same argument applies to lumber. But oil is a limited resource, so for many years predictions have been made (see the previous section) about an impending depletion of the resource. The best-known theory is called Hubbert's Peak.

M. King Hubbert, a geologist who worked at Shell Oil, predicted a worldwide point at which oil production would reach its peak and then begin to decline. This forecasting point is meant to signal when supplies actually start running out. Hubbard presented his ideas in a presentation to the American Petroleum Institute in 1956.[3] Hubbert argued that the rate of oil production would eventually enter a terminal decline, in a period he identified between 1965 and 1970. In 1976, Hubbert revised his estimate by 10 years, citing a flattening of the global production volume by OPEC.

The idea that the world will eventually run out of oil—assuming no changes in production levels, efficiency, or alternative fuel sources—is of course of great concern to any nation consuming imported oil. However, no one really understands the extent of actual reserves, and over the history of the auto and airplane age (only about 100 years old), reserve levels have been updated as ever-higher reserves have been discovered.

However, even though Hubbert's original mathematical models shows U.S. oil production peaking around 1971, this does not *prove* that the theory is either correct or accurate. As a theory developed and based on U.S. oil production, it cannot be applied with accuracy to worldwide reserves and production trends. Since Hubbert's original publication of his theory, numerous new methods of drilling and sources of oil (for example, shale and sand oil) have evolved. Many oil wells formerly capped may be reopened as higher oil prices make extraction economically viable. New discoveries constantly throw estimates off course.

It might be true that the world will eventually run out of fossil fuels, especially if consumption continues to rise. However, production levels are not isolated factors that can be based on a 1956 model, and both economic and political developments affect how, when, and where oil is going to be produced in the future. Hubbert relied on known and proven reserves in 1956, when he announced his ideas. However, among OPEC nations alone, proven reserve levels have been doubled between 1980 and 2006, according to the *BP Statistical Review of World Energy in 2006* (www.bp.com). This known change in reserve levels occurred during a period when oil consumption was also on the rise, which throws Hubbert's estimates into disarray—even though his theories are often cited today as "proof" that world oil supplies are now dwindling.

For oil futures traders, never-ending fear about running out of oil must certainly keep oil prices on the rise. The long-term prospects for oil futures prices are upward and have been for some time. However, on a realistic level the chances of the world running out of energy any time in the immediate future are remote. The development of alternative fuel sources and more efficient automobiles, to name only two obvious developing trends, will further throw Hubbert's estimates off. The trend of predictions between 1914 and 2001 are likely to be more or less duplicated from 2001 through 2100.

How Much Oil Is There?

No one really knows how much oil remains in the ground. However, "proven reserves"—defined as the amount of oil that can be economically recovered—is not even the complete picture. In the future, higher prices are likely to expand the levels of what is economically recoverable, just as lower prices make it less viable to spend money. No oil company or OPEC member is going to spend more money to extract oil than it can get for selling that oil to its customers. Futures traders may not always be aware of the distinction between "proven" and "total" reserves, but the price of oil affects the proven reserve numbers every year. On a more cynical side, observers have been dismayed by the fact that improved fuel efficiency leads to increased auto use, and that means more oil consumption. The picture for long-term energy futures prices is very bullish, especially considering that no effective scenario is on the horizon. In the future, it may be possible to run cars on clean-burning fuel, liquid hydrogen, or solar power. But today, the hybrid models of autos may contribute nothing to the solution, and could even lead to *more* fuel usage, not less.

Table 9-2 summarizes the known world oil reserves and production levels of the most active nations. The estimated supply in terms of years is based on current usage; however, it is clear from this real-world summary that the potential reserves of oil are far from depletion.

It is quite revealing that of total reserves, nearly three-quarters are held by OPEC countries (787 out of 1,059 in billions of reserves, based on the data in Table 9-2). These summaries demonstrate that based on what we know today, we have left at least 40 to 50 years of crude oil supply. And *Oil and Gas Journal* has compiled data indicating that supplies are likely to grow by another 730

TABLE 9.2. OIL RESERVES AND PRODUCTION

Country	Reserves[a] (10⁹ bbl)	Production (10⁶ bpd)	Reserve life (years)
Saudi Arabia	260	8.8	81
Canada	179	2.7	182
Iran	136	3.7	101
Iraq	115	2.2	143
Kuwait	99	2.5	108
UAE	97	2.5	107
Venezuela	80	2.4	91
Russia	60	9.5	17
United States	21	4.9	12
Mexico	12	3.2	10

[a]Estimated reserves in billions (10^9) of barrels (bbl). (Source: *Oil and Gas Journal*, January 2007)
[b]Production rate in millions (10^6) of barrels per day (bpd). (Source: U.S. Energy Information Authority, September 2007)
[c]Reserve life in years, calculated as reserves/annual production.

billion barrels of proven reserves plus yet to be discovered reserves of 938 billion barrels. That is a lot of oil. Factors adding to the optimistic estimates include improved oil recovery technology, past discovery rates, and improved exploration technology. With these estimates in mind, the world has about 100 years of *known* oil reserves available. Oil sand reserves double this to another 100 to 125 years of supply; and oil shale reserves, estimated by the International Energy Agency at over 3.5 trillion barrels, could add another 100 to 115 years of supply.

From an energy futures trading perspective, a plentiful supply of oil reserves could imply that prices are too high, supplies are plentiful, and demand is eventually going to weaken. But reality and perception are not always on the same level of reality. There is a tendency among traders and also among people in general to see things in dire terms. The global warming advocacy community has cited the impending demise of oil (based on updated Hubbert's Peak estimates) as added proof that the world is 10 to 20 years away from self-destruction. The numbers prove otherwise, but futures prices are likely to remain more responsive to widely held beliefs and fears, and less based on actual fact.

Futures Contracts on Energy

The high volume of interest in energy products makes futures trading in oil the highest of any commodity. The light sweet crude contract is the best known and most widely traded. Light sweet and Brent crude oil are both worth mentioning. In addition to crude oil, four additional futures trades are also worth tracking: unleaded gas, heating oil, natural gas, and propane. The following figures show charts for each of these futures contracts as of late December 2007: Figures 9-4 (light crude—March 2008), 9-5 (Brent crude oil—March 2008), 9-6 (unleaded gas—monthly), 9-7 (heating oil—March 2008), 9-8 (natural gas—March 2008), and 9-9 (propane—March 2008).

The price history of crude oil has been volatile, due not only to the supply and demand of the market, but also to geopolitical changes and threats. The oil embargo of 1973, which halted shipments of oil to the Western countries in retaliation for support of

FIGURE 9.4. LIGHT CRUDE OIL—MARCH

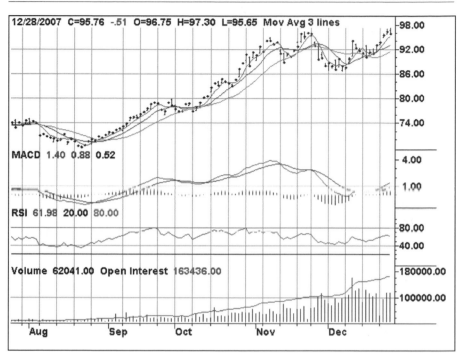

Source: Charts provided courtesy of TradingCharts.com: http//futures.tradingcharts.com; created with SuperCharts by Omega Research © 1997.

Israel in the Yom Kippur War, caused prices to soar above $100 per barrel (inflation-adjusted for 2008 price levels). This led to long gas lines, double-digit interest rates and inflation, and overall global tensions. These did not ease until after 1980, when the embargo had been lifted and Middle East tensions quieted down. In the 1990–1991 invasion by Iraq of neighboring Kuwait, fast action by the United States ended the invasion, but oil prices rose along with the tension. Even with periodic increases in oil production among OPEC countries, concerns about greater demand and perceptions of a dwindling worldwide supply add to ever-growing oil prices. Developing countries—notably China—add to the overall demand, further pressuring oil and futures prices upward.

Besides crude oil and its derivatives, any emerging markets for alternative energy also trade in futures. Biodiesel and ethanol are among the most promising of the non–fossil fuel sources. Ethanol is

FIGURE 9.5. BRENT CRUDE OIL—MARCH

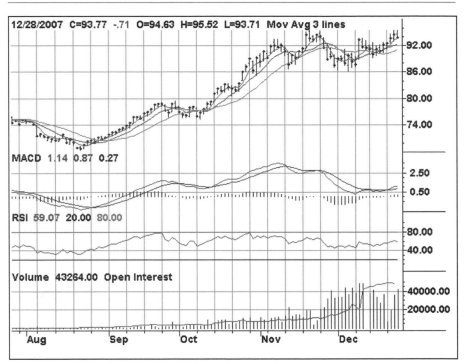

Source: Charts provided courtesy of TradingCharts.com: http//futures.tradingcharts.com; created with SuperCharts by Omega Research © 1997.

controversial, however. Current cost of production makes it more expensive than crude oil and it also drives up food and feed prices. Ethanol can be manufactured from numerous agricultural products, the most popular being corn and sugar. In Brazil, sugar cane–based ethanol is used widely, and in the United States the trend is more likely to focus on corn, due to growing patterns and climate. However, widespread use of these agricultural products directly affects futures value of both sugar and corn, anticipating near-term increases in food and livestock feed prices as well. The December 2007 contract for March ethanol traded as shown in Figure 9-10.

Biodiesel is derived from vegetable oil, including soybean, canola, and palm oils. This product is used as a substitute for home heating oil and diesel fuel. But just as ethanol affects the prices of corn and sugar, increased demand for biodiesel will have a similar effect on the vegetable oil used in its production. Additional re-

FIGURE 9.6. UNLEADED GAS—MONTHLY

Source: Charts provided courtesy of TradingCharts.com: http//futures.tradingcharts.com; created with SuperCharts by Omega Research © 1997.

search continues into additional agricultural-based uses, including products not used so widely as food and feed sources not widely used directly for food. These include potential fuel development from corn stalks, switch grass, and hay.

Chapter 10 covers another large futures industry, grains and oilseeds. Agricultural products are crucial to the United States as well as import and export partners, and a lively and complex futures market reflects this reality.

Notes

1. R. J. Pirlot, "The Time Is Now: Tap Arctic Oil Reserves," *Wisconsin Manufacturers & Commerce,* www.wmc.org, also citing data from www.anwr.org.
2. EIA, *Annual Energy Outlook 2006,* February 2006.
3. M. King Hubbert, "Nuclear Energy and the Fossil Fuels," Spring Meeting of the Southern District, American Petroleum Institute, March 7–9, 1956.

FIGURE 9.7. HEATING OIL—MARCH

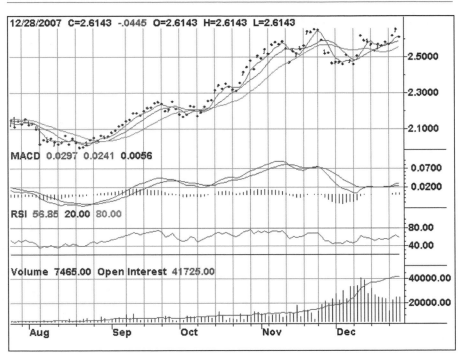

Source: Charts provided courtesy of TradingCharts.com: http//futures.tradingcharts.com; created with SuperCharts by Omega Research © 1997.

FIGURE 9.8. NATURAL GAS—MARCH

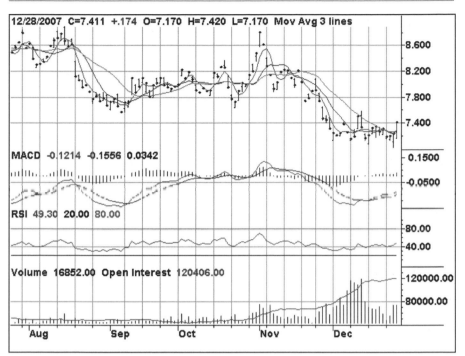

Source: Charts provided courtesy of TradingCharts.com: http//futures.tradingcharts.com; created with SuperCharts by Omega Research © 1997.

FIGURE 9.9. PROPANE—MARCH

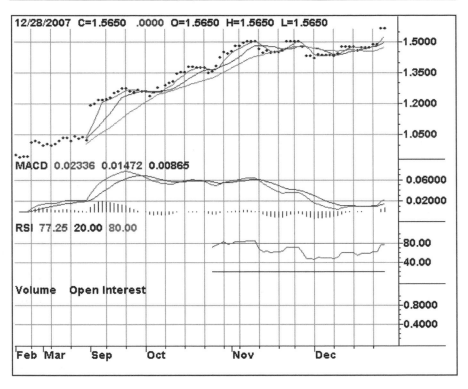

Source: Charts provided courtesy of TradingCharts.com: http//futures.tradingcharts.com; created with SuperCharts by Omega Research © 1997.

FIGURE 9.10. ETHANOL—MARCH

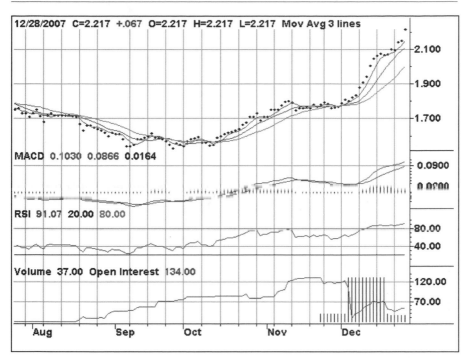

Source: Charts provided courtesy of TradingCharts.com: http//futures.tradingcharts.com; created with SuperCharts by Omega Research © 19997.

AGRICULTURE

A broad range of agricultural products accounts for a very active volume of trading in U.S. futures markets. This segment includes grains and oils in nine major categories: corn, wheat, rice, cotton, oats, soybeans, Western barley, canola, and lumber.

Lumber is included in the agricultural segment because it is grown and harvested; and it is replenished by replanting. The majority of agricultural products serve as food and feed, and lumber is the one exception to this. The complexity of agricultural futures makes this segment especially interesting. It cannot be viewed in isolation. For example, corn and oats affect futures prices in other major futures segments. Both are used as feed for cattle, so the livestock segment is going to rise or fall as corn and oat prices change. In addition, with increased interest in development of ethanol as an alternative fuel, corn has found a *third* demand. Besides food and feed, corn is also the base crop for ethanol in the United States. In South America, sugar is the preferred crop, and different climates account for the difference in the two regions. This chapter describes the broad markets and uses for each of the agricultural commodities, and provides price charts as of the end of December 2007 for March 2008 contracts.

▨ Corn

The corn crop is one of the most significant, not only in the United States but worldwide. Four states—Iowa, Illinois, Nebraska, and Minnesota—grow more than half of the entire U.S. corn crop. Additional states—Indiana, Ohio, Wisconsin, South Dakota, Michigan, Missouri, Kansas, and Kentucky—are added to the four major states to form what is known as the U.S. corn belt.

The United States is also the largest producer of corn in the world. Exported corn—about one-fourth of all corn grown in the United States—is used primarily as livestock feed, and the Pacific Rim region—where a majority of humans live—is the fastest growing market for U.S.-grown corn. The uses of corn as food and feed are only the most obvious and recognized uses. Within the food group, corn has multiple uses. As a *starch*, corn is used in food as well as in production of drugs, cosmetics, and industrial manufacturing. Industrial uses include development of adhesives, batteries, bookbinding, cleaners, coatings, dyes, fireworks, crayons, chalk, cardboard, plastics, refinery of oil and ore, lubricants, paint, wallpaper, tires, surgical dressings, and textiles.

Corn is used for various *food* products, not only well-known corn products such as corn on the cob and canned corn, but also in baby food, bakery products, beer, chewing gum, confections, powered sugar, pancake mix, flour, mustard, pudding, salad dressing, soup, pet food, and sauces.

Corn used for *drugs and cosmetics* include antibiotics, aspirin, body lotion, drug coatings, lipstick, makeup, soaps, and cleansers.

Corn also is applied in creation of *dextrose*, crystalline sugar made from corn starch and enzymes. Also called corn sugar, dextrose has many industrial uses, including amino acids, adhesives, dyes, enzymes, biodegradable products, leather tanning, lysine, paper, rubber, and textiles.

Another variation is *corn syrups*, which are applied not only to food products but also to industrial applications such as ink, dyes, rayon, shoe polish, and metal plating. Corn also is essential for *solubles*, made from water and softened corn. The resulting steepwater is needed for production of antibiotics, chemicals, pharmaceutical drugs, and yeast. On the industrial side, solubles are used to make chemicals, insecticides, varnish, rubber substitutes, and livestock feed. Food solubles include cooking oil, margarine, mayonnaise, salad dressing, and snack food products. *Protein and fiber* developed from corn include animal feed from gluten meal. Corn fiber is also used to manufacture gluten feed for beef and cattle foods. Corn *germ* is also used for animal feed, and germ is also converted to corn oil.

Corn has so many uses that it would be difficult to imagine the overall effect on so many products if the corn crop were reduced. The cost of corn will rise as ethanol uses continue to expand, however. This means that all of the food, industrial, and other applications of corn products may suffer higher prices in the future due to more and more corn crops being used for fuel production. Corn prices are also affected directly by direct causes:

- The availability of other livestock feed commodities, such as soy meal and wheat
- Loans and subsidies from the government
- Weather, especially dry spells
- The harvest size of corn crops in Argentina and Brazil as well as other export rivals
- The count of the livestock and poultry market for which corn is used as feed

The corn futures chart for the March contract is shown in Figure 10-1.

Note the strong uptrend between October and December. During this period, oil prices were rising and approaching $100 per barrel, aggravated by Middle East tensions. During this period, interest in production of ethanol was very much in the news. These kinds of trends demonstrate that corn prices are subject not only to demand for food and feed, but also by the potential energy shortages, whether real or perceived, that have so much impact on the U.S. economy.

The RSI approached the overbought mark toward the end of this period, indicating an overvalued condition. Additionally, MACD also showed an upward momentum. Technicians would be inclined to see these trends in a bearish way, and anticipate a price decline. How-

FIGURE 10.1. CORN—MARCH CONTRACT

Source: Charts provided courtesy of TradingCharts.com: http//futures.tradingcharts.com; created with SuperCharts by Omega Research © 1997.

ever, the added ethanol factor could have a bullish effect on corn prices, depending on the extent of production, tax credits, and food/feed prices as the ethanol debate moves forward. The price of oil is also a factor directly influencing corn prices. For example, if oil prices were to decline, that could soften the demand for higher volume of ethanol production, softening the demand for corn as well.

As with all commodities, the spectrum of market influences work together to determine price direction. Corn, more than most commodities, has so many applications within the agricultural sector and in others (livestock and energy), that price trends are especially difficult to anticipate. There are many variables.

Wheat

Second in growth volume only to corn, wheat crops are among the most important in the world. Wheat grows worldwide and in several varieties. It is a staple food for making flour, bread, cookies, noodles and other pasta, cakes, and couscous. It is also fermented to make beer and alcohol. Wheat can also be used as a biofuel. A secondary value to wheat is as a forage crop for livestock.

The broad dependence on wheat crops as a primary food source accounts for its price strength in the futures market. Any negative outcome in conditions, including freezes, droughts, and exceptionally short growing seasons, affects supplies worldwide. As a consequence, prices rise. With this in mind, it is doubtful that wheat prices are likely to decline on a permanent basis in the future.

The science of wheat breeding and expansion is complex. Objectives include high yield, resistance to disease and insects, and weather tolerance. Major species include *common wheat*, also called bread wheat. This is the most commonly grown form of wheat in the world. Other varieties include durum, einkorn, emmer, and spelt. In the commodities market, wheat grain is classified by properties to determine price levels. In 2007, futures prices spiked in the wheat market due to freezes and floods in the northern hemisphere and a serious drought in Australia.

The demand for wheat is strong worldwide. Global consumption averaged 101 kilograms per person in 1997.[1] Wheat consumption in China is one-sixth of the total worldwide consumption, and, whereas rice grows only in limited climates, wheat grows in many regions, making it a more reliable food staple. Most varieties of wheat require 110 to 130 days from planting to harvest, varying by climate, soil conditions, and type.

According to the United Nations Food and Agriculture Organization (*www.fao.org*) wheat shortages are not uncommon, especially in third world countries, where wheat production is highest and dependence on wheat is greatest. Wheat production as of 2005 (measured in millions of metric tons) was:

Country	Production
China	96
India	72
United States	57
Russia	46
France	37
Canada	26
Australia	24

Germany	24
Pakistan	22
Turkey	21
Other nations	201
World Total	626

In the United States, several subclasses of wheat are popular. These include durum, hard red spring, hard red winter, soft red winter, hard white, and soft white. Each of these varieties is used in specific food and other end uses.

Figure 10-2 shows the December 2007 chart for March 2008 wheat contracts.

▓ Rice

After corn and wheat, the third most important crop worldwide is rice. Although these other crops are more widely used, many parts

FIGURE 10.2. WHEAT—MARCH CONTRACT

Source: Charts provided courtesy of TradingCharts.com: http//futures.tradingcharts.com; created with SuperCharts by Omega Research © 1997.

of Asia depend on rice as a major food source. These regions are characterized by high rainfalls and a plentiful supply of water. As a crop, rice provides 20% of worldwide calorie intake.

Rice growth requires planting of seeds, followed by flooding of the field. Proper planning and soil conservation requires careful drainage and channeling as well as careful control of hearty weeds, insect pests, and disease, especially in the submerged field areas. Rice can be grown without the flooding approach, but these other approaches demand higher levels of weed and pest control in growth seasons as well as a more complex fertilization method.

In addition to the well-known use of rice as a daily food, raw rice is also ground into flour and then used for production of rice milk and sake (rice wine), as well as many varieties of noodles. However, even though it is used as a primary food in many regions, rice is not a complete protein, meaning it does not contain a full range of essential amino acids. Rice can be puffed (or popped) by heating the pellets and then used as a source for cereal grains and other foods.

Rice has been grown in the United States since the seventeenth century, when it was introduced in the Carolinas. The southern states grew large volumes of rice during the seventeenth and eighteenth centuries, with production accelerated after invention of the rice mill and the use of water power. With the end of slavery after the Civil War, rice production was less profitable. At the time of the California Gold Rush of 1849, rice cultivation became widespread, with the use of Chinese immigrant labor. By 2006, the upper San Joaquin Valley (six counties north of Sacramento) was the second most productive rice growing area in the United States, after Arkansas.

Production worldwide of paddy rice crop, as reported by the United Nations Food and Agriculture Organization, measured in millions of metric tons, was:

Country	Production
China	182
India	137
Indonesia	54
Bangladesh	40

Vietnam	36
Thailand	27
Myanmar	25
Pakistan	18
Philippines	15
Brazil	13
Japan	11
Other nations	142
World Total	700

This growth level reflects a strong rise in worldwide production since 1960, when production was only 200 million metric tons per year. Exports are relatively small, however, with only about 5% of all rice sent to other countries. The three largest rice exporters are Thailand (26% of exports), Vietnam (15%), and the United States (11%). The three largest importers of rice are Indonesia (14%), Bangladesh (4%), and Brazil (3%). Most paddy rice is used domestically, especially in Asia. In Cambodia, for example, 90% of the total agricultural land area is used for rice production.

These realities indicate continuing strong markets for rice worldwide. Because it is a primary food in so many heavily populated regions (notably those with growing population levels), rice will continue to report strong price support into the future.

Figure 10-3 summarizes the December 2007 chart for the March 2008 rice contract.

Note the October through December strong rise in price levels, accompanied with the Relative Strength Index (RSI) remaining below 80. This indicates that the price level remained reasonable and had not moved into "overbought" areas.

Cotton

Few commodities have had as much effect on U.S. economic history than cotton. In the nineteenth century, the expression "Cotton is king" had great significance, and the differences between the industrial north and the agricultural south had much to do with the roots of the Civil War. Before gold was discovered in California in 1849, cotton was the chief consumer product not only domestically but also as an export.

FIGURE 10.3. RICE—MARCH CONTRACT

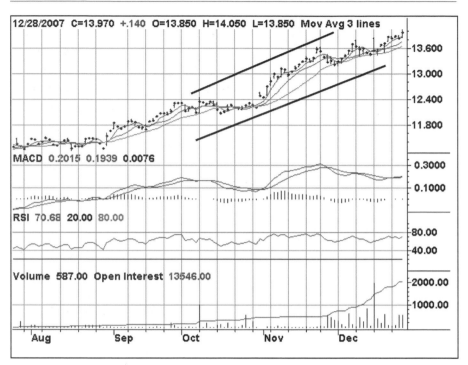

Source: Charts provided courtesy of TradingCharts.com: http//futures.tradingcharts.com; created with SuperCharts by Omega Research © 1997.

It all happened in only a few decades. In 1800, the United States did not produce cotton. By 1860, the south was exporting five-sixths of the world's cotton, over 2 billion pounds every year. One author observed that this industry "was then about as important as the oil industry in the Middle East today . . ."[2] The Civil War, the causes of which were varied and complex, caused a sudden upward spike in cotton prices, and speculators ran prices upward and downward for many years to come.

By 2007, the three leading cotton-producing countries were China, India, and the United States. Leading exporters of cotton were the United States, Uzbekistan, and India. In the United States, Texas led in overall production, but California had the highest yield per acre of cotton crop. Because cotton requires an abundance of sunshine, long periods without frost, and adequate rainfall, seasonally dry areas are most productive for cotton harvesting.

Genetically modified (GM) cotton is used worldwide as a substitute that overcomes pesticide use for naturally grown crops. In 2002, 20% of the world's cotton was GM; by 2003, GM cotton was 73%. One of the greatest rates of growth in GM cotton occurred in India. In 2002, India yielded 50,000 hectares of cotton, but by 2006 India was producing 3.8 million hectares, or 76 times more than only four years before. Today, India has more GM cotton than any other country, including China.

Looking back, eighteenth century innovations in Great Britain enabled the industrial revolution to go into high gear. Among the most important inventions were the spinning jenny, the spinning frame, and the flyer-and-bobbin system for drawing cotton to a uniform thickness. In the United States, Eli Whitney's cotton gin made production even easier and faster. However, these inventions also led to a decline in cotton labor, as manual harvesting was replaced by machinery. Today, cotton is among the U.S. major exports, notably from the southern state region.

Cotton is used primarily in textile manufacturing; most people also recognize the cotton fibers in clothing as a primary element in blends. Cotton also is used to manufacture denim, corduroy, seersucker, terrycloth, and twill. Most socks, underwear, and T-shirts are also cotton, as well as a majority of bedding products.

Beyond clothing, cotton is also used widely to knit and crochet and blended with rayon and polyester. Other industries rely on cotton as well, and it is used to manufacture fish netting, coffee filters, gunpowder, paper, and tents. Cottonseed is used to produce cottonseed oil. Shiny cotton, a processed variety, is used to manufacture clothing resembling satin, and is used in shirts as well as suits. In Asia, cotton is used to manufacture mattresses, common to that region.

U.S. production of cotton is not on par with other countries, and 25,000 cotton growers in the United States are subsidized, with the government paying approximately $2 billion per year. A change in these subsidies could affect domestic cotton prices, as well as continued trends in other countries to dominate the production and export of cotton. Given the potential for less viable markets in the future (for example, if the subsidies were stopped), the futures market for cotton is not as strong as that for commodities used as food and manufacturing products and in continuing and growing demand.

Figure 10-4 summarizes the December 2007 chart for March 2008 cotton.

Note the roller coaster of price ranges in the last few months of 2007. However, with the variance of eight points, both MACD and RSI indicated that the price range was within reason, based on those technical standards. This points out the value of supplementing price information with technical tests, also indicating that cotton's futures price trends can offer short-term speculative opportunities.

FIGURE 10.4. COTTON—MARCH CONTRACT

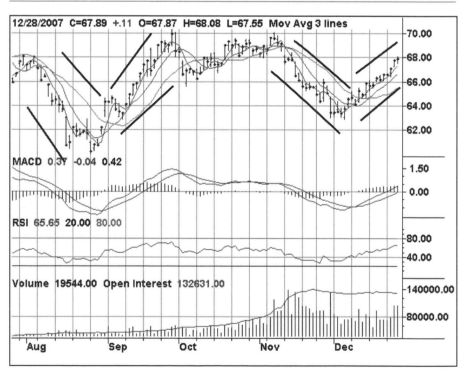

▧ Oats

The most significant cereal grain is the oat grain. However, it is equally important as a source of livestock feed, for both horses and other cattle. Oats are also used in production of dog food and are widely used as chicken feed. As such, oats futures prices also directly affect livestock futures.

Oats grow in most temperate zones and do well with relatively low summer heat compared to other grains. Oats also are more tolerant of high rainfall compared with wheat, rye, and barley. So cooler, wet summers in countries of northwest Europe (including Great Britain and even Iceland) do not prevent successful oat crops.

Oat bread was first introduced in England, and today oats are used as a main ingredient in Scottish diets. In fact, the famous lexicographer Samuel Johnson defined oats as "a grain, which in England is generally given to horses, but in Scotland supports the people."[3]

According to the UN Food and Agriculture Organization, worldwide production as of 2005 (in millions of metric tons) was:

Country	Production
Russia	5.1
Canada	3.3
United States	1.7
Poland	1.3
Finland	1.2
Australia	1.1
Germany	1.0
Belarus	0.8
China	0.8
Ukraine	0.8
Other nations	7.5
World Total	24.6

Oats are used in many types of food. Rolled or crushed, they become oatmeal or can be ground into oat flour. Products include porridge, oatcakes, cookies, muesli, and granola. In Great Britain, a variety of beer called oatmeal stout includes oats for the wort. In

Scotland, the husks of oats are soaked and the remaining floury meal strained off and boiled to make a dish called sowans.

Dehulled and rolled oats are used as feed for horses, and whole or ground oats are also used as cattle feed. Oat straw is also used in skin conditioners and lotions. Figure 10-5 shows a chart for the March 2008 contract as of December 2007.

Soybeans

Three distinct futures contracts trade on this product: soybeans, soy meal, and soy oil. Each has its own distinct uses and applications.

Most soy crop is extracted for conversion to oil, and soy meal is primarily used for livestock feed. A relatively small amount of soy crop is used directly as food for humans, but this varies regionally

FIGURE 10.5. OATS—MARCH CONTRACT

Source: Charts provided courtesy of TradingCharts.com: http//futures.tradingcharts.com; created with SuperCharts by Omega Research © 1997.

with most consumption occurring in Asian regions (for example, soy sauce, tempeh, and miso). Soy is also used in a number of processed foods. In the United States, soy was first used in the late eighteenth century, grown for hay as livestock feed. However, outside of Asia, soy did not become used widely until early in the twentieth century.

Soybeans grow best in climates with hot summers. When mean temperatures fall under 68 degrees Fahrenheit, growth of soy falls off. Even though uses of soy as a food product are mostly found in Asia, the United States is the world's leading producer. According to the UN Food and Agriculture Organization, major soy producers as of 2005 (in millions of metric tons) were:

Country	Production
United States	83.9
Brazil	52.7
Australia	44.7
Argentina	38.3
China	17.4
India	6.6
Paraguay	3.5
Canada	3.0
Bolivia	1.7
Other nations	62.5
World Total	314.3

The United States is also the leading exporter of soybeans. One market factor affecting futures prices in the future will be environmental concerns. Greenpeace and the World Wildlife Federation claim that soybean cultivation has destroyed large areas of Amazon rainforest. As green policies become more prevalent around the world, the effect on soy prices could be substantial. Brazil has the second highest production of soybeans in the world, so even if cutbacks in growing areas were to be limited to Brazil alone, it would impact world supplies significantly.

In the United States, soybeans are among the so-called biotech foods, and have been genetically modified for many uses. For example, in 1995 "Roundup Ready" soybeans were introduced, which cannot be killed by the popular active ingredient in Roundup. This allows farmers to spray the herbicide without losing valuable crops, while reducing weeds in soy fields. Before 1997, only 8% of U.S.-grown soy was genetically modified. By 2006, 89% were GM soy.

Vegetable-type uses of soybeans include production of tofu, soy flour, and soy milk (it is not actually milk, but is widely referred to as milk). As an oil, soy has a high protein content (38% to 45%). Soybeans are the leading agricultural export in the United States, which is encouraging for futures traders because international demand supports continued expansion of the U.S. crop.

Soy meal is what remains after extraction of the soy flakes and is used for defatted soy flour. This product contains under 1% oil. Full-fat soy flour is produced from unextracted, dehulled soy beans, and has about 20% oil content. Low-fat soy flour is produced by adding back a portion of oil to defatted soy flour. And high-fat soy involves adding higher levels of oil.

One widespread use of soy as a human food source is infant formula. This use is especially useful for lactose-intolerant infants or those allergic to milk protein. These products are sold in powdered or concentrated liquid form. Soybeans are also used to produce nut butter, a less fattening peanut butter substitute. Soy is also used to produce margarine, soy yogurt and cheese, cooking fat (like Crisco), and many other substitutes for popular foods.

Nonfood uses of soybeans include manufacture of soap, cosmetics, resin, plastic, ink, crayons, solvents, and clothing. It is also a potential biodiesel fuel base, and is used as fermenting stock to produce vodka.

Figures 10-6, 10-7, and 10-8 show the March 2008 contracts for soybeans, soybean oil, and soybean meal as of December 2007.

Note the soybeans trend. Prices rise steadily throughout the second half of the year, but the RSI level also rose and reached 80. This indicates the contract was close to overbought. The soybean oil showed a very similar trend. Soybean meal contracts showed the same tendency, but at the end of the chart period, price and RSI both dropped off.

FIGURE 10.6. SOYBEANS—MARCH CONTRACT

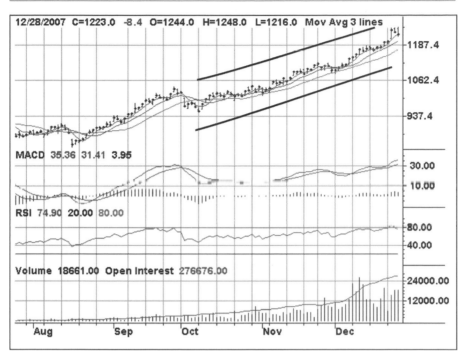

Source: Charts provided courtesy of TradingCharts.com: http//futures.tradingcharts.com; created with SuperCharts by Omega Research © 1997.

■ Western Barley and Canola

Barley is a leading cereal grain as well as livestock food crop and malting base. Barley is second only to wheat in importance and uses. However, barley is more expensive to produce and more sensitive to varying soil conditions. The UN Food and Agriculture Organization reported the top barley producers as of 2005 (in millions of metric tonnes):

Country	Production
Russia	16.7
Canada	12.1
Germany	11.7
France	10.4
Ukraine	9.3

FIGURE 10.7. SOYBEAN OIL—MARCH CONTRACT

Source: Charts provided courtesy of TradingCharts.com: http//futures.tradingcharts.com; created with SuperCharts by Omega Research © 1997.

Turkey	9.0
Australia	6.6
United Kingdom	5.5
United States	4.6
Spain	4.4
Other nations	47.7
World Total	*138.0*

Uses of barley are different than most other grains. About half of total production is applied to livestock feed and a large portion of the remaining production is used for malting of beer and whiskey, as well as nonalcoholic products like barley water and mugicha (a popular drink in Japan and Korea). In Europe, barley is a very popular ingredient in soup and stew.

Western barley is a futures trade, based on production in Alberta, Canada. This is the source for nearly half (44%) of Canada's

FIGURE 10.8. SOYBEAN MEAL—MARCH CONTRACT

12/28/2007 C=333.5 -10.4 O=346.5 H=347.6 L=332.0 Mov Avg 3 lines

340.0
320.0
300.0
280.0
260.0
240.0

MACD 10.97 10.62 0.35

12.00
4.00

RSI 63.62 20.00 80.00

80.00
40.00

Volume 10448.00 Open Interest 109598.00

10000.00
5000.00

Aug   Sep   Oct   Nov   Dec

Source: Charts provided courtesy of TradingCharts.com: http//futures.tradingcharts.com; created with SuperCharts by Omega Research © 1997.

total barley crop (Saskatchewan produces 35% and Manitoba produces 12%). Much of the Western barley from Alberta is exported to overseas markets, but the majority remains in Canada and is used as livestock feed.

Most of the Western barley produced trades on the cash market, but the Western barley contract (traded on the Winnipeg Commodity Exchange) has seen increased volume in recent years as price variations make cash markets less certain.

Barley has become one of Canada's most important crops. In the 10 years ending 2005, Western barley averaged over 12 million metric tonnes, the second highest volume in the world. Because a large portion of Western barley is used as livestock feed, barley serves multiple purposes in the futures market. Barley prices affect prices of livestock, as well as malted beverages. To a lesser degree, changes in barley prices also affect food prices, especially in Europe where barley is most popular.

Figure 10-9 shows the December 2007 chart for March 2008 Western barley.

Note the large price run-up in August and September, accompanied by signals in both MACD and RSI; and then the price retreat confirmed by the same technical signals.

The origin of the word canola is "**Can**adian **O**il, **L**ow **A**cid." It was developed first in 1978 and is also known as lear oil (**L**ow **E**rucic **A**cid **R**apeseed). GM canola oil is resistant to herbicides, and today 80% of Canadian-grown canola is of the GM variety. Canola is also Australia's third largest crop and is used by wheat farmers as a break crop to improve quality of soils. (A "break crop" is a secondary crop used in crop rotation, to break the cycle of weeds, infestations, and diseases.) In the United States, over 90% of canola is produced in one state, North Dakota. In addition to its

FIGURE 10.9. WESTERN BARLEY—MARCH CONTRACT

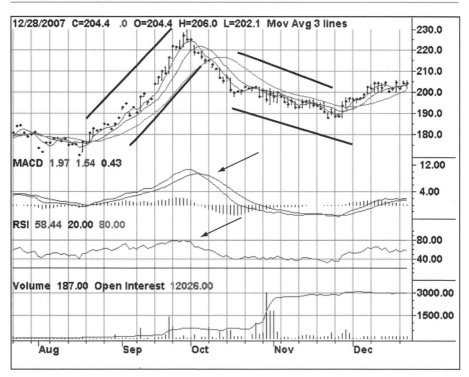

Source: Charts provided courtesy of TradingCharts.com: http//futures.tradingcharts.com; created with SuperCharts by Omega Research © 1997.

primary use in cooking, canola has potential as a biodiesel fuel. Canola futures trade on the Winnipeg Commodity Exchange.

Figure 10-10 shows the March 2008 canola contract as of December 2007.

Note the price rise in November and December, and the movement of RSI approaching 80, a signal that the trend was approaching overbought conditions.

■ Lumber

While lumber is not usually considered part of the agricultural futures classification, it is included here. The product is planted, harvested, and renewed. These attributes give lumber enough in common to be treated as an agricultural commodity.

Lumber is well-known for its uses in construction. It is also essential for production of wool pulp and paper products. Pulp-

FIGURE 10.10. CANOLA—MARCH CONTRACT

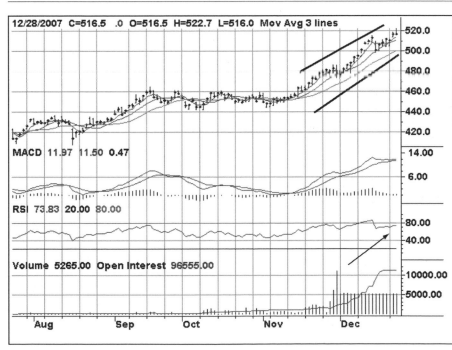

Source: Charts provided courtesy of TradingCharts.com: http//futures.tradingcharts.com; created with SuperCharts by Omega Research © 1997.

wood (rough lumber) is used as a raw material for furniture manufacturing. Finished lumber is milled in standard sizing and is used primarily in the construction business. Popular softwoods include pine, cedar, fir, spruce, and hemlock.

Engineered lumber is designed for very specific uses. These include laminated veneer lumber (LVL), which are doubled or tripled up and provided in longer lengths for use as structural beams. This product is necessary where dimensional lumber would not be structurally strong enough to provide adequate support and where spans are too long for other products. Wood I-joists (also called trus joists) are used in flooring, or as piers in flooring foundations. Manufactured trusses are used for the construction of roofs, providing faster and easier construction and support than other methods. Oriented strand board (OSB) consists of strands of thin wood glued together to improve strength. OSB is a replacement for plywood and used for exterior walls, flooring, and decking. In flooring, it often includes the popular tongue-and-groove design.

For futures trading, one important factor significantly affecting lumber prices is an ongoing dispute between the United States and Canada. Mostly affected has been Canada's westernmost province, British Columbia, where a majority of softwood lumber exports are produced. U.S. claims that the Canadian lumber industry is priced unfairly due to federal and provincial subsidies is at the core of the dispute. In fact, the Canadian government owns most of Canada's timber resources. Harvest prices (stumpage fees) are set by administrative decision rather than in the competitive market. This affects not only market prices but futures contract prices as well. This dispute has been going on since 1982.

Figure 10-11 shows the March 2008 lumber contract as of December 2007.

A four-month price decline in the last months of 2007 was accompanied by RSDI falling below 40, a signal that the contract may be undersold at that point.

For additional information on agricultural futures, trends, and useful statistics, check:

National Grain and Feed Association, www.ngfa.org

USDA National Agriculture Library, www.nal.usda.gov

FIGURE 10.11. LUMBER—MARCH CONTRACT

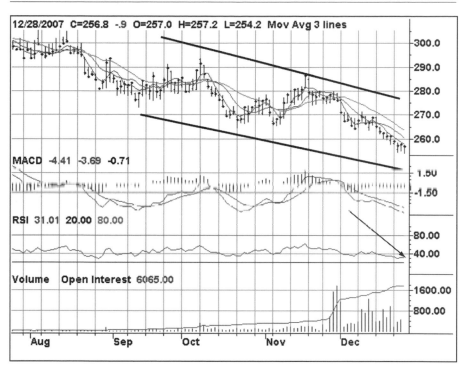

Source: Charts provided courtesy of TradingCharts.com: http//futures.tradingcharts.com; created with SuperCharts by Omega Research © 1997.

USDA, at www.usda.gov

USDA National Agriculture Statistics Service, www.nass
.usda.gov

The next chapter moves into livestock futures, which often are affected directly by crop cycles and prices.

■ Notes

1. International Grain Council, "Grain Market Report," and Centro Internacional de Mejoramiento de Maiz y Trigo (CIMMYT), World Wheat Overview and Outlook, 2000-2001 (www.CIMMYT.org).
2. Marc Faber, *Tomorrow's Gold* (Hong Kong: CLSA Books, 2003).
3. Samuel Johnson, *Dictionary of the English Language* (1755).

CHAPTER 11

LIVESTOCK

The overall importance of livestock—including all meat products used for food and dairy production—represents about one-fifth of the typical family's monthly budget (according to the USDA).[1] The costs going into livestock businesses include not only the cost of acquisition of the product, but feed and marketing costs as well. Feed, a factor of the agricultural market, is going to vary in cost with corn, wheat, oats, barley, and other feed sources. If corn crops, a major feed source, are used increasingly for ethanol production, then the cost of corn is going to rise; and that means the cost of livestock will rise as well, and those costs will be reflected in futures prices even before they hit the family pocketbook.

More than most other futures contracts, livestock futures tend to be extremely volatile. This is due to the feed costs, competition, and seasonal factors affecting what it costs to feed livestock and deliver the final product to market. That means transportation costs also affect livestock, not to mention the expected cycles, weather, and current trends in the marketplace. For example, in past years fear about mad cow disease, which began to affect livestock in Great Britain, caused a considerable price change in the U.S. livestock futures market. Demand fell rapidly as consumers stopped buying beef products, and restrictions in the livestock import/export market aggravated the situation.

There is little doubt that future volatility in livestock prices will continue, for a variety of reasons. In this chapter, four major futures are examined: live cattle, feeder cattle, lean hogs, and pork bellies.

▧ Live Cattle Futures

Cows have served as a major food source for centuries, not only for beef but also for a range of dairy products. Industries based on cattle marketing are vast. The Chicago Mercantile Exchange (CME) began offering live cattle futures contracts in 1964, representing the first such contract on a living animal.

Because livestock cannot be stored indefinitely, the turnaround in the market is relatively short. This may add to the volatility in live cattle futures, but supplies of meat also affect prices, and that is going to vary based on numerous factors. For example, in some years the herd number will be higher or lower than average, based on perceptions of market demand, feed costs, and other factors. But herd expansion—the process of creating more livestock— takes five to seven years to be realized, based on breeding cycles and the need to select out females for breeding rather than for slaughter. So during periods of herd expansion, long-term product increases but short-term supplies fall. In periods of herd contraction, the opposite effect is seen. Short-term availability increases as more livestock are slaughtered, although long-term availability is intentionally reduced. Herd contraction may take as much as four years to complete the cycle.

So in the livestock market, the futures prices vary considerably not only as a result of current supply and demand, but also based on future capacity. The decision to expand or contract herd size is based on a producer's estimates of profitability, and that is always a factor of costs, primarily the costs of feed. During periods when feed prices rise, profitability declines. This reality demonstrates that most commodities are intertwined and move as a consequence of one another. The costs associated with energy, agriculture, and livestock are the primary cause-and-effect futures for this reality.

Ranchers in the beef industry make important decisions in their cow/calf operations. Cows breed in late summer, and birthing is a spring event. This beef industry is focused in a few states with potentially great temperature swings, especially in winter. So the states between Texas and Montana are the primary base for the cycle of cow/calf production. Weather also affects the grazing patterns of beef and accounts for some seasonal movement of cattle from one locale to another.

Calves are weaned from 6 to 10 months after birth, when they reach a "feeder weight" between 600 and 800 pounds. They are then classified as feeder cattle (more about this in the next section). Thus, it takes as long as 18 months between breeding and slaughter. During that time, producers have to consider feed costs, disease prevention, and other costs associated with developing their market.

Most U.S.-produced live cattle is consumed domestically. Trade restrictions affect exports, and in recent years, Japan and South Korea have curtailed imports of U.S. beef, based on fears of mad cow disease. Before this disease was first diagnosed in a U.S. cow in 2003, $1.7 billion of exports to Asian countries per year was a major activity. In 2006, a third case of mad cow disease continued the ban on beef in Asian markets.

These factors make live cattle an uncertain futures contract. However, the popularity of beef and dairy cannot be denied, and live cattle represent a strong and high-volume market, although futures prices are anything but certain. Figure 11-1 shows the April 2008 contract for live cattle as of December 2007.

■ Feeder Cattle

Feeder cattle futures have been available on the CME since 1971. By definition, feeder cattle are calves weighing between 600 and 800 pounds. Once calves attain weight in this range, they are moved to feedlots for fattening and slaughter. The futures contract is priced based on the *CME Feeder Cattle Index*, representing the averages of seven-day cash prices from the largest producing states. These 12 states are Colorado, Iowa, Kansas, Missouri,

FIGURE 11.1. LIVE CATTLE—APRIL CONTRACT

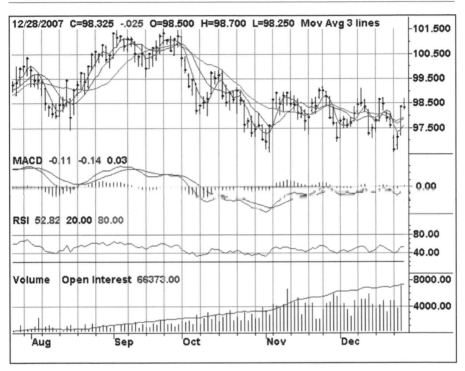

Source: Charts provided courtesy of TradingCharts.com: http//futures.tradingcharts.com; created with SuperCharts by Omega Research © 1997.

Montana, Nebraska, New Mexico, North Dakota, Oklahoma, South Dakota, Texas, and Wyoming. For information about how the average is calculated, check the CME link at *www.cme.com/files/calculationCMEFeederCattle.pdf.*

Feeder cattle prices vary based on the herd levels in prior years, which of course affects the number of calves in the current year. To fatten stock, grain is needed; so grain prices directly impact feeder cattle and, as a result, meat prices in coming months.

Figure 11-2 shows the April, 2008 contract as of December 2007.

Note the price decline over the period shown, as well as the RSI. This dipped below the threshold of 40 a few times and ended the period slightly above. This indicator shows that the price decline is close to oversold levels.

FIGURE 11.2. FEEDER CATTLE—APRIL CONTRACT

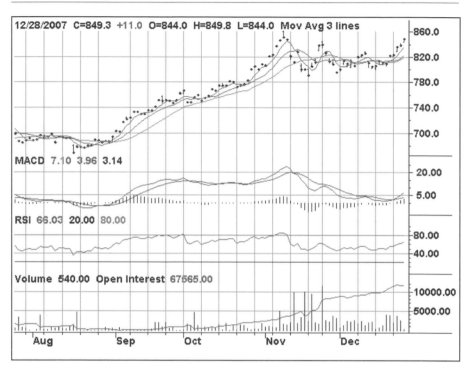

Source: Charts provided courtesy of TradingCharts.com: http//futures.tradingcharts.com; created with SuperCharts by Omega Research © 1997.

Lean Hogs and Pork Bellies

The futures contract for lean hogs (a more civilized name for hog carcasses) has traded on the CME since 1997. Both producers and import/export businesses use the contract, which was initiated to replace live hog futures traded previously. Since the market trades in lean hogs, it makes sense to trade in this form rather than in futures based on value of the live animals.

The lean hogs contract is quite volatile. Because this contract is used more by producers than by speculators, it is less liquid than many other futures contracts. In addition, according to a survey conducted by the University of Missouri, as of 2006 (http://agebb .missouri.edu/mkt/porkind06.ppt#20), the number of small hog producers in the United States has decreased, while the number of large-scale operations has increased dramatically. The study revealed a change since 1988, when hog farms with fewer than 1,000

head represented 32% of the entire market share, and larger
(50,000+) farms were only 7% of the market. In 2006, those operations with less than 1,000 head fell to 1%, while the larger farms
rose to 43%:

Herd Size (thousands)	% of Total Market
under 1	1%
1–10	14
11–50	21
51–500	21
Over 500	43
Total	100%

In addition to market share, the number of hog farms in the
larger volume portion of the market grew as well. From 1994 to
2006, the study showed:

Year	Number of Farms		% of Slaughtered Hogs	
	50–500	Over 500	50–500	Over 500
1994	57	9	7%	10%
1997	127	18	13	24
2000	138	20	17	35
2003	149	24	20	39
2006	164	27	21	43

As smaller hog farms represent a shrinking portion of the market,
prices also fell. In 1997, futures prices of lean hogs were $83.55
per pound; in 1999, they had fallen to $20.70. By the end of 2007,
prices had returned to a range between $60 and $70.

The market resides mostly in five states: Iowa, Minnesota, Illinois, Indiana, and Ohio. Production also affects the market price.
Average gestation for hogs is 114 days, and litter size is about 10
piglets. It takes more than six months for hogs to reach a market
weight of 250 pounds. So with the breeding season starting in the
spring, the highest volume of slaughter takes place in the fall.

The lean hogs futures contract includes end market products
including ham, pork chops, and lunch meats. In comparison, pork
bellies consist mainly of bacon, and futures contracts were first of-

fered by the CME in 1961. This was the first futures contract for slaughtered livestock; other futures trading involved live animals until that time. Both markets are robust in today's market, as consumption levels have risen. Today, hog products contain about half the fat content of 50 years prior. Another factor affecting demand is the growing fast food industry, where high volume of sales includes many products such as bacon (hamburgers and breakfast menus). The United States is the world's largest exporter as well, with more exports going to Japan than any other nation. Another factor helping pork markets is increased concern about mad cow disease, negatively affecting beef demand.

Figure 11-3 shows the lean hogs April 2008 contract as of December 2007.

Note the steady price decline from September through December. The RSI level had fallen below 40 on numerous occasions, and

FIGURE 11.3. LEAN HOGS—APRIL CONTRACT

Source: Charts provided courtesy of TradingCharts.com: http//futures.tradingcharts.com; created with SuperCharts by Omega Research © 1997.

ended the period under that level. This indicates that the contract may be oversold at that point.

Figure 11-4 shows the pork bellies contract with a March 2008 delivery date as of December 2007.

The pork bellies contract was quite volatile in this five-month period. Note that at the end of both price declines, RSI fell below the 40 level. Thus, the contract was oversold at both of these low points. The November price growth confirms this indicator.

The next chapter continues an examination of futures contracts with precious metals, including six important contracts: gold, silver, copper, aluminum, platinum, and palladium.

▨ Notes

1. USDA Economic Research Service, "Food Consumption: Household Food Expenditures," February 5, 2008.

FIGURE 11.4. PORK BELLIES—MARCH CONTRACT

Source: Charts provided courtesy of TradingCharts.com: http//futures.tradingcharts.com; created with SuperCharts by Omega Research © 1997.

PRECIOUS METALS

M etals serve many uses in many markets. Futures contracts respond to metals as a form of currency, for manufacturing, jewelry, medicine and dentistry, and many other important and essential applications. This chapter summarizes six important precious metals in terms of market use and futures contracts. Beyond these, numerous other metals can be traded, bought and sold directly, or invested in through ETFs.

Among ETFs, gold and silver draw the most interest. Gold ETFs include streetTRACKS Gold Shares (GLD), iShares COMEX Gold Trust (IAU), Market Vectors Gold Miners (GDX), and PowerShares DB Gold (DGL). Silver ETFs include iShares Silver Trust (SLV) and PowerShares DB Silver (DBS). Many other ETFs include portfolios mixing precious metals and including metals and other futures contracts.

■ Gold

Before the 1970s, the U.S. currency conformed to the gold standard, meaning the currency in circulation was limited by gold reserves. Before 1934, a troy ounce of gold was valued by the United

States at $20.67. In 1934, this was raised to $35 per ounce. On March 17, 1968, a two-tiered pricing system was set, keeping the international settlement price at $35 per ounce but allowing the market price to fluctuate. Although the United States did borrow additional funds beyond reserves, its ability to accumulate debt was inhibited by the gold standard. Today, the largest gold reserve is maintained at the New York Federal Reserve Bank, which has approximately 3% of all the gold ever mined. Another large deposit is held at Fort Knox, Kentucky.

Today, the gold standard is not used as the basic international exchange, and although the U.S. dollar is widely used as the international currency of choice, the vulnerability of currency values has become a matter of concern in the futures market and elsewhere. Today, gold serves not as a standard for valuation, but often as an alternative to currency. When speculators are worried about the safety of currency, they often move investment dollars into gold, through direct ownership of bullion, shares of gold mining companies, ETFs, or gold futures.

Many countries use gold for coinage, and minting creates potential investment value as the price-per-ounce of gold rises over time. Most coins have been minted in 22k weight, also called crown gold, since pure gold of 24k is too soft for this application. Among the popular gold coins in circulation today are the Canadian Gold Maple Leaf, the Australian Gold Kangaroo, and the American Buffalo. However, gold coins hold more interest among coin collectors and gold speculators than for use as currency. Coins such as the American Gold Eagle and British Gold Sovereign have strong market interest among coin enthusiasts.

In addition to its importance as an alternate form of currency, gold is used in a broad range of applications, notably dentistry and electronics. Gold's features include a high resistance to corrosion, so it is the preferred metal for such applications. Gold also forms easily with other metals to form alloys. This enables manufacturing and industrial applications to expand the use of gold in their products and processes.

In electronic applications, gold is an excellent heat and electricity conductor and, because it is resistant to corrosive effects of heat, moisture, and oxygen, gold is by far the preferred metal in jewelry.

Jewelry manufactured with gold is alloyed with many other metals, usually silver, copper, iron, aluminum, palladium, and nickel. Gold solder is used in jewelry manufacturing.

Interest in gold on many levels has persisted for centuries. Gold has been considered a healthy alternative medicine in many cultures and has been believed to have healing powers. Today, gold has been shown to have anti-inflammatory properties and gold salts are often included in medicines to treat arthritis. Gold leaf and gold dust are also used in some gourmet foods as decorative features. This is derived from the belief in gold's healing power as well as the desire among wealthy hosts to show off their ability to use gold in this manner. An herbal liqueur found in Germany is called *Goldwasser* (Goldwater), and contains gold flakes. The flakes add no nutritional value to the water, but the drink is a popular status symbol.

Dentistry relies on gold for construction of crowns, bridges, and fillings. The gold alloy used for these applications is malleable but produces better results than the porcelain crowns of the past.

Gold production is concentrated in a few areas of the globe. About one-half of all gold in the decades between 1970 and 2007 was mined in South Africa. In 2007, China became the world's leading gold producer. Other major gold finds have occurred in the United States, Australia, Russia, and Peru. About two-thirds of all gold used within the United States comes from mines in South Dakota and Nevada. Additional large reserves of gold exist in the world's oceans, but it is not economically possible to extract it. On average, extraction costs $238 per troy ounce.

Gold prices are set on the gold fixing standard, based in London since 1919. The London Bullion Market Association (www.lbma.org.uk) sets the gold fixing; it publishes fixing for gold and silver as well as U.S. and U.K. forward valuation. According to the LBMA, "The fixings are an open process at which market participants can transact business on the basis of a single quoted price. Orders can be changed throughout the proceedings as the price is moved higher and lower until such time as buyers' and sellers' orders are satisfied and the price is said to be 'fixed.'"[1]

Prices vary based not only on supply and demand, but on perceptions of political unrest and threats to currency values. So gold and its value on the futures market reacts to a multitude of market factors and perceptions, not the least of which is the level of actual and known gold reserves. In 2005, the World Gold Council (www .gold.org) estimated total worldwide gold supply at 3,557 tonnes and total demand at 3,386 tonnes. Of the demand level, 81% is used to manufacture jewelry.

The United States holds more than twice the reserves of any other country (8,135 troy ounces as of 2006), followed by Germany (3,427 ounces), and the International Monetary Fund (3,217 ounces). Besides popular use in jewelry, physical ownership of gold is a popular idea. Investors and speculators hold gold in the form of coinage, gold bars (from 1 gram up to 400 troy ounces), and gold certificates, held in place of the actual gold, which is held for investors by the company or country issuing the certificates. The Perth Mint (*www.perthmint.com.au*) is the most authoritative source for finding approved dealers and issuers of gold certificates.

Price levels of gold are reflected in futures prices as speculators attempt to estimate the direction and speed of future price increases. On January 21, 1980, gold prices reached an all-time high of $850 per ounce, but retreated to a record low on June 21, 1999, of $252.90. The older high price record was surpassed in March 2008, when the gold futures contract moved above $1,000 per ounce, to quickly retreat by June 2008 to about $850. These prices reflect absolute dollar values; the previous highs of the 1980s were much higher when adjusted for inflation.

Figure 12-1 shows price levels as of December 2007 for the April 2008 gold 100 ounce contract.

Silver

After gold, silver is the most widely used precious metal. Its attributes include the highest electrical conductivity of any element. The majority of silver is mined as a by-product of mining for other metals, notably gold, copper, lead, and zinc.

Silver has also been popular as a metal used in coinage, jewelry, and tableware. Major world producers are Peru and Mexico. In 2005, Peru mined one-seventh of all the silver mined worldwide. Peru's production in 2006 was 102.6 million ounces, followed by

FIGURE 12.1. GOLD (100 OZ.)—APRIL CONTRACT

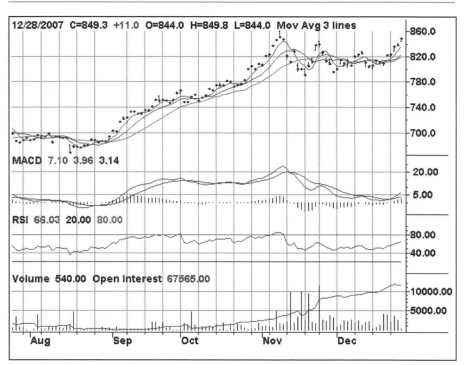

Source: Charts provided courtesy of TradingCharts.com: http//futures.tradingcharts.com; created with SuperCharts by Omega Research © 1997.

Mexico (92.3 ounces), Australia (77.4 ounces), and China (64.7 ounces).

Grades differ based on use. Well-known sterling silver contains 92.5% silver and 7.5% copper. An alternative, Britannia silver, has a higher silver content at 95.8%; this is used widely for production of silverware and wrought plate products. The metal is also used to manufacture musical instruments and as an amalgam for dental fillings and crowns. The high conductivity of silver makes it popular in the manufacture of electrical and electronic goods as well, including printed circuits, which use silver paint, and computer keyboards with their silver contacts. Silver is the most popular metal used in solder and brazing, as well as in silver-zinc and silver-cadmium batteries.

As a currency, silver has been the most popular metal of choice for many centuries. The words for "silver" and "money" are identical in more than 10 languages, and in Great Britain the unit of currency, the pound, is derived from the original value base of one troy pound of sterling silver. Investors can purchase silver coins or 100 ounce silver bars.

Silver also has a history in medicinal uses. Before the invention of antibiotics, silver compounds were used to prevent infections, for treatment of severe burns, and in wound dressings. Today, silver compounds are found in many remedies. However, excessive use of silver in medicines has caused cases of argyria in which the skin turns bluish-gray. Other possible side effects such as coma have also occurred.

Figure 12-2 shows the 5,000 ounce silver contract for March 2008 as of December 2007.

FIGURE 12.2. SILVER (5,000 OZ.)—MARCH CONTRACT

Source: Charts provided courtesy of TradingCharts.com: http//futures.tradingcharts.com; created with SuperCharts by Omega Research © 1997.

▣ Copper

Copper is a required nutrient for all life forms and, even though it is found in the bloodstream of humans, high levels can be poisonous. This element is valuable for electrical and heat conductivity and is used in many building materials. High reserves of copper in the United States have kept prices fairly low, and Chile also holds high reserves of copper. Mining in the United States has been active since the early 1700s. The oldest operating copper mine in the United States is in Vermont. The Elizabeth Mine (The "Liz") was closed in 1958. Significant mining continues today in Utah, Nevada, and Tennessee.

Construction uses of copper include piping for water supplies and heating systems; copper wire use in electrical systems; and for lead-free solder. The Statue of Liberty contains nearly 180,000 pounds of copper. It is also used in shipbuilding and in the manufacture of waterproof roofing material and rain gutters. In technological applications, copper is replacing aluminum as the metal of choice for integrated circuits. Cookware and flatware often are constructed of copper. Sterling silver, used for flatware, contains copper as well.

Coinage has used copper as an alloy or alternative to silver. Currencies in Europe (the Euro), the U.K., Australia, and New Zealand all use copper. In the United States, copper is among the most popular metals, notably in the penny and nickel (the U.S. nickel is constructed of only 25% nickel, and 75% copper).

Figure 12-3 shows the March 2008 futures contract for high-grade copper as of December 2007.

▣ Aluminum

A major advantage to industrial, aerospace, and transportation uses for aluminum is its exceptional resistance to corrosion. Aluminum is among only a few metals that retains its luster in powdered form, making it valuable for use in paint. It is also in demand for electrical and electronic uses, as an effective thermal and electrical conductor.

Although the most abundant metallic element on earth, alumi-

FIGURE 12.3. COPPER (HIGH GRADE)—MARCH CONTRACT

Source: Charts provided courtesy of TradingCharts.com: http//futures.tradingcharts.com; created with SuperCharts by Omega Research © 1997.

num is rare in free form. This explains the popularity of aluminum recycling. Scrap is melted for reuse, a process taking up only 5% of the energy required to mine new aluminum. Aluminum production costs include 20% to 40% of the cost spent in electric power. So aluminum is very expensive to extract. Major smelting countries are China, Russia, Canada, the United States, South Africa, New Zealand, and Australia. China produces one-fifth of the total world supply. The metal is widely used in aircraft production due to its high strength-to-weight ratio, and it is formed into alloy with copper, zinc, and silicon as well as other elements.

In addition to use in aircraft, aluminum alloys are used in the manufacture of automobiles, railway cars, ships, and bicycles. It is also a primary packaging material used to make cans and foil. In construction, aluminum is popular for production of windows, siding, and doors. Additional uses include cookware, household wiring, and electrical transmission lines. In its purest form (99.9%), aluminum is used to make CDs and DVDs.

One important drawback of aluminum alloys, when compared to steel, is a high fatigue factor. Aluminum alloys will fail eventually, so that aluminum products have a limited life. These alloys are also heat-sensitive, and will melt easily. Operations like welding and casting are difficult and lead to internal stress.

Figure 12-4 shows the March 2008 contract as of December 2007.

Note the large downtrends occurring at two points in this chart. Both concluded with RSI dropping beneath 40, a clear signal that the contract was oversold.

Platinum and Palladium

Platinum is a heavy, malleable, ductile metal highly resistant to corrosion. It is widely used in jewelry, electrical contact equipment,

FIGURE 12.4. ALUMINUM—MARCH CONTRACT

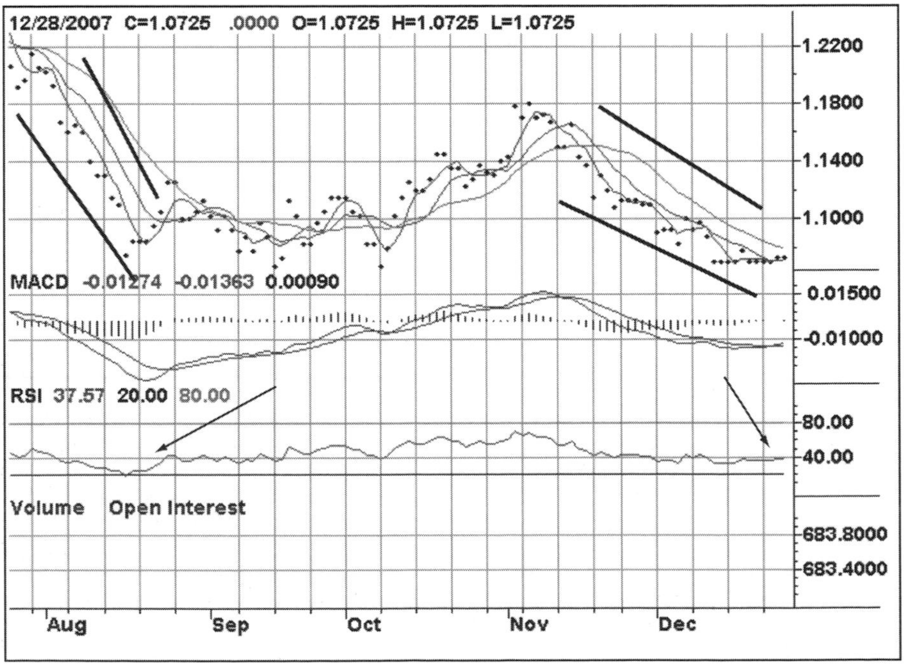

Source: Charts provided courtesy of TradingCharts.com: http//futures.tradingcharts.com; created with SuperCharts by Omega Research © 1997.

dentistry, auto emissions control devices and catalytic converters, spark plugs, as a catalyst in fuel cells, in watchmaking, and in laboratory equipment.

Platinum is very rare, estimated to be 30 times more rare than gold. South Africa is the world's leading platinum miner, accounting for 80% of the world supply. Second- and third-place producers are Russia and Canada. In 2006, the total world supply was only about 7 million troy ounces; U.S. futures prices rose strongly in the last half of 2007, mirroring the rise of gold prices during the same period, and prices of many other precious metals.

Figure 12-5 shows the April 2008 contract as of December 2007. The price rose steadily, reaching approximately $1,550 per ounce. By the following month, platinum prices rose to record high levels, up to $1,634.50 by January 25, 2008.

Note that although prices rose strongly, the RSI remained under 80, indicating that the price was reasonable for this contract and was not overbought.

FIGURE 12.5. PLATINUM—APRIL CONTRACT

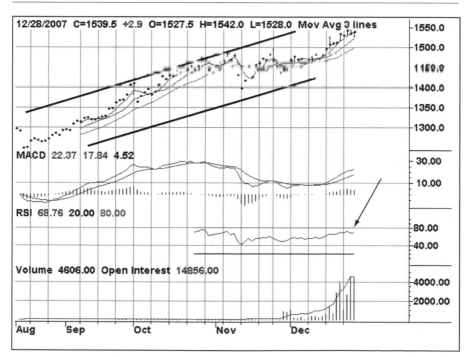

Source: Charts provided courtesy of TradingCharts.com: http//futures.tradingcharts.com; created with SuperCharts by Omega Research © 1997.

Palladium is a rare metal very similar to platinum in structure. It is most often mined as an extraction by-product of copper and nickel ores. It is a viable alternative to platinum because its value is one-third to one-fourth of platinum's per-ounce cost.

The top world producer is Russia, which mines more than half of the world supply. Other countries mining palladium include South Africa, the United States, and Canada. It is used widely in electronics, soldering, catalytic converters, and in the manufacture of jewelry, as well as in dentistry, watchmaking, spark plugs, and surgical instruments.

Figure 12-6 shows the March 2008 contract for palladium as of December 2007.

Note the bottom at the start of December accompanied by very high volume, and a dip in RSI below 40—and then a reversal and price increase to the end of the month.

FIGURE 12.6. PALLADIUM—MARCH CONTRACT

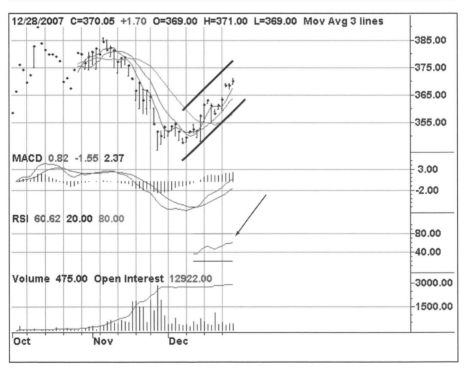

Source: Charts provided courtesy of TradingCharts.com: http//futures.tradingcharts.com; created with SuperCharts by Omega Research © 1997.

Chapter 13 continues the discussion of futures contracts with a look at imports and tropical products.

▨ Notes

1. www.lbma.org.uk, link "about the fixings" on "statistics" page.

					5 Yr. Treasury Not
June					111-087 111
Sept					113-165 110
					2 Yr. Treasury Note
					June	106-037 106-<
					30 Day Federal Fund
					April	97.735 97.7<
					May	97.943 97.96
					1 Month Libor (CME)-\$:
					May	97.2100 97.230(
					June	97.2850 97.2950
					Eurodollar (CME)-\$1,000,0
					May	97.1450 97.1925
					June	97.1200 97.2150
					Sept	97.0400 97.1500
					Dec	96.8600 96.9700
					Currency Futures

Currency Futures

CHAPTER   13

IMPORTS AND
TROPICAL PRODUCTS

C ommodities that are imported from other countries, also called "tropicals," may be quite volatile due to global effects of interest rates, currency exchanges, and geopolitical events. This chapter describes and analyzes four primary imports and tropicals—coffee, sugar, orange juice, and cocoa.

■ Coffee

Among beverages of choice, coffee is one of the most popular. This is true not only in the United States, but worldwide. The early success of companies like Starbucks and smaller, more localized retailers and roasters has made coffee more popular than ever. As of early 2008, McDonald's began installing coffee kiosks in many of its retail food outlets, competing head to head with more expensive Starbucks locations. The popularity of coffee is unlikely to fall off at any time in the near future. About 1.6 billion cups of coffee are consumed every day worldwide. Even with the popularity of soft drinks, coffee provides about 54% of caffeine intake.

Coffee beans are imported from Africa, Southeast Asia, the Middle East, and South America. By the year 2000, 6.7 tonnes of coffee were produced per year, and by 2010, the number is expected to rise to 7 tonnes. Among exporters, Brazil is the largest coffee producing country, with Vietnam second and Columbia third. Four companies well-known in the United States buy about half of all coffee produced annually. These companies are Kraft, Nestlé, Procter & Gamble, and Sara Lee. This high volume of demand provides a healthy floor for coffee production, and although different blends are in use by smaller sources of demand, the high volume of use provides stability in the coffee market. Futures trading has also been affected by fair trade labeling, providing guarantees to coffee growers of negotiated minimum prices. Fair trade certification is widely believed to have had a positive impact on both producers and consumers.

Coffee takes three to five years from planting to harvest, which at times causes imbalances in supply and demand. Farmers tend to plant when coffee prices are high, even though the lead time until harvest is so long. Production levels have grown steadily at more than 2% per year since the 1970s. The International Coffee Organization (www.ico.org) and the National Coffee Association (www.ncausa.org) provide statistics about the coffee market and trends among producing countries and coffee consumption.

The International Coffee Organization reported that for 2007, the three major producers accounted for more than half of worldwide production in 2007. In thousands of bags of coffee, these were:

Country	Bags (in thousands)	Percent
Brazil	33,740	29%
Vietnam	15,950	14
Columbia	12,400	11
All other	53,776	46
Total	115,866	100%

Each bag of coffee weighs 60 kilograms, or about 132 pounds, so these totals represent significant production and exporting activity worldwide. Two varieties dominate the market. About 60% of all coffee is arabica, a premium coffee bean with a rich brewed taste. This serves as the benchmark for coffee pricing worldwide, based on its quality. The remaining 40% is robusta, which is less expensive. Coffee futures contracts are traded on the New York Board of Trade (NYBOT) and involve arabica prices only. The distinction is important because of price differences. The coffee futures contract is properly called Pure Arabica Coffee.

Figure 13-1 shows the March 2008 contract as of December 2007.

The trading range at this time was between 120 and 140 (per contract size of 37,500 pounds), a range that has held for the past decade. However, prior to 1998, prices were far more volatile, and went as high as about 300 briefly. The volatility of coffee prices is at the mercy of weather and the long planting-to-harvest time.

■ Sugar

Two major varieties of sugar are traded through futures contracts. Sugar #11 is raw sugar produced worldwide, and sugar #14 is

FIGURE 13.1. COFFEE—MARCH CONTRACT

Source: Charts provided courtesy of TradingCharts.com: http//futures.tradingcharts.com; created with SuperCharts by Omega Research © 1997.

raw sugar produced only in the United States. It is widely used not only in good and food preparation, but also in industrial applications. Sugar futures are the second most actively traded commodity on the NYBOT. Sucrose (also known as table sugar) is produced from both sugar cane and sugar beet. It can be dissolved in water to form syrup, and dissolved sugar is widely used in foods. Worldwide production exceeds 134 million tonnes. Cane sugar is produced in warm climates, and major producers include Brazil (30 million tonnes per year), India (21 million), China (11 million), as well as Thailand, Mexico, and Australia (about 5 million tonnes each). Beet sugar can be grown in cooler climates such as northern Japan and parts of the United States.

Because the United States has set high prices for imported sugar as a means of domestic price supports, many countries have begun using corn syrup in place of sugar. Sweeteners like glucose syrup used in beverages and candy can also be derived from wheat and corn. Artificial sweeteners are used in many soft drinks as well. These trends threaten traditional markets for sugar, and as trade competition dominates the market due to climatic differences between producing and consuming nations, the trend toward seeking sugar alternatives will probably continue. The United States is not the only country that subsidizes domestic sugar production. The European Union and Japan practice this too.

The World Trade Organization (www.wto.org) ruled in 2004 that many of the tariffs and artificial price supports practiced worldwide were illegal. The EU responded by cutting sugar prices 39% and doing away with all sugar exports. Further reforms in trade practices are likely to occur into the future. A small portion of specialty grades of sugar are designated as "fair trade" commodities. However, competition by region has caused a price war in the form of premiums offered to smaller farmers, and a series of sugar protocols. The U.S. Sugar Program and the ACP (African, Caribbean, Pacific) Sugar Protocol (www.acpsugar.org) have offered premiums of $400 per tonne above world market prices. Meanwhile, the Sugar Association (www.sugar.org) has begun a campaign promoting sugar use over artificial substitutes.

These international competitions and price wars make sugar futures trading interesting and volatile. Politics certainly affects sugar prices, and the United States continues to impose a quota on imports. This keeps domestic sugar prices well above worldwide prices, and as with all artificial price supports, may cause a shake-out in the future.

Figure 13-2 shows the March 2008 contract for sugar #11 as of December 2007.

▓ Orange Juice

The primary orange juice futures contract in the United States is traded in the form of frozen concentrate, and is called Frozen Concentrated Orange Juice (FCOJ). The juice is pasteurized prior to freezing. There are three forms of juice:

1. Reconstituted single-strength orange juice is sold as a ready-to-drink form sold in bottles or cartons without requiring refrigeration.

FIGURE 13.2. SUGAR #11—MARCH CONTRACT

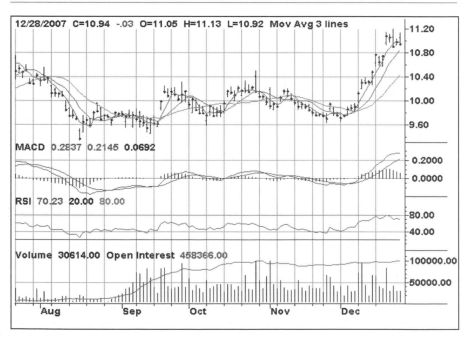

Source: Charts provided courtesy of TradingCharts.com: http//futures.tradingcharts.com; created with SuperCharts by Omega Research © 1997.

2. Not-from-concentrate juice is pure-form juice. It is pasteurized and processed and none of the water content of the juice is removed.
3. The FCOJ juice has to be defrosted and reconstituted before use. This is the form of juice traded on the futures market. Since oranges are perishable, the frozen form is advantageous because it can be stored and transported.

Oranges grow in many countries. However, only two locations—São Paulo, Brazil, and Florida—have processing facilities able to handle a large volume. These two locations dominate the market, with over 90% of world orange production. It takes an orange tree three to four years between planting and the first harvest. São Paulo trees average 20 years productivity; Florida's trees are productive up to 40 years. However, exceptionally hard frosts can destroy trees. In Florida, the additional threat of hurricanes also poses a serious threat.

Florida suffered a hard freeze in 1962, destroying much of the season's crop and tree inventory. Up until that time (from the 1940s to 1960s) Florida had been the only major world producer of oranges. After 1962, São Paulo began competing with the Florida market. Today, Brazil dominates production, with the United States producing about half as many tons. Other major producers include Mexico, India, Italy, China, Spain, Iran, Egypt, and Indonesia. Germany, Britain, and France also produce oranges, but on a reduced scale due to weather differences with the Florida market. Increased production in Russia and Eastern Europe has made this region more competitive with other minor markets, including Japan, Australia, and South Korea.

Figure 13-3 shows the orange juice contract for March 2008 as of December 2007.

Cocoa

The most common variety of cocoa is called Forastero, which represents 95% of worldwide production. A second variety, Criollo, is harder and more expensive to produce. Cocoa is not necessarily processed where it is produced, nor does consumption level occur

FIGURE 13.3. ORANGE JUICE—MARCH CONTRACT

Source: Charts provided courtesy of TradingCharts.com: http//futures.tradingcharts.com; created with SuperCharts by Omega Research © 1997.

in production or processing countries. The Netherlands is the leading cocoa processor, followed by the United States. Switzerland, Belgium, and the United Kingdom have the highest consumption levels.

Production levels have grown over the past few decades. In 1974, worldwide production was about 1.6 tonnes. By 2004, this level had grown to 3.7 tonnes, an increase of over 130% in 30 years, according to the International Cocoa Organization (www .icco.org).

According to the UN Food and Agriculture Organization, production leaders (in million tonnes) in 2004 were:

Country	Cocoa Production (in millions tonnes)
Ivory Coast	1.33
Ghana	0.74
Indonesia	0.43
Nigeria	0.37

Brazil	0.17
Cambodia	0.13
Ecuador	0.09
Other	0.34
Total	3.60

Cocoa is processed to produce chocolate, cocoa butter, candy, soap, and cosmetics. In the futures market, potential problems include farming problems due to poor education in many of the highest-volume regions. Sustainable farming methods in these areas is one of the major objectives of public/private partnerships sponsored by the World Cocoa Foundation (www .worldcocoafoundation.org). Another issue that has led to worldwide concern is the use of child slavery in the leading producing nation, the Ivory Coast. The U.S. State Department estimated that more than 100,000 children were exploited in 2002 in this manner. This problem has led to a U.S. sponsored Cocoa Protocol, aimed at reducing the U.S. purchase and use of cocoa grown in countries using forced child labor. Today, a certification program is in use, aimed at ensuring that cocoa imported from Africa is not produced in this manner.

Most of the world's supplies come from African nations, and an intergovernmental organization, the Cocoa Producers' Alliance (www.copal-cpa.org), represents the interests of growing countries. The organization's Web site lists four objectives: exchange of technical and scientific data; advance social and economic relations between producing nations; ensure adequate supplies for the market; and expansion of cocoa consumption.

The market is limited due to climatic constraints. Cocoa trees grow only within 20 degrees from the equator, and best conditions are with temperatures from 66°F to 92°F. Rainfall must be high as well, and the combination of shade and humidity is ideal. Thus, the potential for expansion of the cocoa crop is geographically difficult. Due to the high potential for political unrest in many of the third world countries where cocoa is grown, the futures market for cocoa is likely to experience volatility as events unfold.

Figure 13-4 shows the March 2008 futures contract for cocoa at December 2007.

FIGURE 13.4. COCOA—MARCH CONTRACT

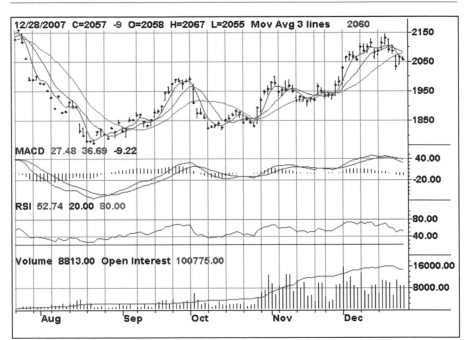

Source: Charts provided courtesy of TradingCharts.com: http//futures.tradingcharts.com; created with SuperCharts by Omega Research © 1997.

The next chapter departs from commodity futures to explain the various kinds of futures contracts on financial instruments (interest rates and currency), individual stocks, and indices.

```
5 Yr. Treasury Not
June    111-087 111
Sept    113-185 110
2 Yr. Treasury Note
June    106-007 106-0
30 Day Federal Fund
April   97.735  97.7
May     97.920  97.90
1 Month Libor (CME)-5
May     97.2100 97.2900
June    97.2850 97.2950
Eurodollar (CME)-$1,000.0
May     97.1450 97.1925
June    97.1200 97.2150
Sept    97.0400 97.1500
Dec     96.8600 96.9700
Currency Futures
```

FINANCIAL, INDEX, AND STOCK FUTURES

n addition to the many different commodities on which futures can be traded, one very large segment of the futures market is for the noncommodity areas: financial (interest rates and currency futures), indices, and individual stocks. This chapter explains all these variations.

Commodities are at the center of the world economy, and trading in energy, agriculture, livestock, precious metals, and imports affects every aspect of life. However, everyone is also subject to the economic forces affected by international debt, interest rates, currency policies, and actions taken by central banks (including the U.S. Federal Reserve). It would be reasonable to define noncommodity futures as types of commodities. In a sense, stocks and money are commodity-like in some of their attributes; and futures trading in these instruments often works much like futures on physical commodities. However, because shares of stock, currency rates, interest, and other financial futures are not physical, it also makes sense to treat them separately.

Financial-type futures trading has existed only since the 1970s. Today, traders and institutions use financial futures to hedge other positions. Institutions and corporations can use interest and currency futures to protect against losses or to augment profits, and many applications are possible. For example, a company with a lot of overseas business activity may be concerned about currency exchange losses. Using currency futures to protect against that possibility is one practical and common method for protecting net profits at a relatively small cost. Companies with a lot of cash on their books often invest funds in securities for a few months or years. However, many debt obligations are at risk of declining in value. Based on ever-changing rates, a bond's face value may fall to a discount, and losses are possible, especially if the company will need to liquidate these holdings within the short term. So to protect against the possibility of declining value, the long position in a debt instrument can be hedged with a short position in the same instrument (for example, Treasury notes or bonds). So if the long position's value falls, it will be offset by a decline in the short futures position, so that at the time of liquidation, the short position profit will offset the long position loss.

The intriguing aspect of using short futures to hedge against long positions, either in debt instruments or stocks, is that as prices evolve, the relative values change as well. Because futures decline in value over time, the tendency is to approach zero by the delivery date. The hedge position ends up creating net gains because of this, regardless of whether the prices of the underlying commodity move up or down. In comparison, a long hedge (where you buy a long futures contract to hedge against a short position) is more likely to create a loss, also due to the declining value of the futures trade as the delivery date approaches.

These are only examples of many possible hedging and speculative strategies using financial futures. Individuals can also use financial futures through options or with futures on stocks, leveraging capital while gaining a controlling position in the underlying security. The variety of financial futures available expands your possibilities for short-term profits, hedging, risk mitigation, and speculation.

Interest Rate Futures

As the name implies, a futures contract for interest rates is based on the rate assessed or charged by an issuer. Because money supply is constantly changing, rates charged for commercial bonds and government bonds also are subject to auction and to competitive forces. Because the rate of bonds is fixed, the current value of bonds may also move at a premium above face value or at a discount below face value. This affects the current rate of a bond as well.

Interest rates affect the entire economy and may also predict inflation or even recessions. As companies expand operations, they borrow money and pay competitive rates for long-term debt capitalization. As the federal and state governments fund their projects and operations, they issue bonds as well. In the futures market, many benchmark interest rates change with time. The Federal Reserve, which is the U.S. central bank, sets reserve requirements for member banks and establishes federal funds and discount rates. Fed member banks function through its open market operations. The Federal Open Market Committee (*www.federalreserve.gov/fomc/fundsrate.htm*) buys and sells Treasury securities, which also is the focus of many key futures contracts. There is much more to the interest futures market, of course. Trading also takes place in mortgage interest rates, for example. The very first interest rate futures contract began on October 12, 1975, on futures of Ginnie Mae (Government National Mortgage Association, which creates mortgage pools made up of residential home mortgages, also referred to as the mortgage secondary market).

Futures trading exists on both short-term and long-term interest rates. Short-term includes 2-year Treasury notes, the Eurodollar, 30-day Federal Funds rate, and 1-month London Interbank Offered Rate (LIBOR) futures. Long-term futures contracts include 5- and 10-year Treasury notes and Treasury bonds futures.

The government-based futures are on instruments issued by the federal government to fund the national debt and ongoing government operations. So these Treasury bills, notes, and bonds are the funding mechanism for the entire U.S. government. Government debt instruments come in a range of terms, including 3- and 6-month Treasury bills, 2-, 5- and 10-year Treasury notes, and Treasury bonds (these were discontinued in 2001). Even though the long-term bonds—30 years from issue to maturity—have been discontinued, the existing bond contracts prior to that time are still in effect, and active trading in outstanding T-bonds is ongoing.

There is also an active futures market for the 30-year T-bond futures contract. Figure 14-1 summarizes one of the many interest futures contracts, the March 2008 contract as of December 2007.

■ Currency Futures

The currency of each country or region changes very regularly, and futures contracts track values from one currency in relation to another. On any given day, a conversion rate applies. This means that one unit of currency in one country is worth another amount in the other. For example, the U.S. dollar is equivalent to various other currencies. Comparisons to the British pound, the euro, and the Japanese yen as of February 11, 2008 were:

	British Pound	Euro	Japanese Yen
1 USD is worth:	0.5131890	.68937	106.64
currency in USD:	1.9486	1.4506	0.00937734

FIGURE 14.1. 30-YEAR U.S. TREASURY BONDS—MARCH

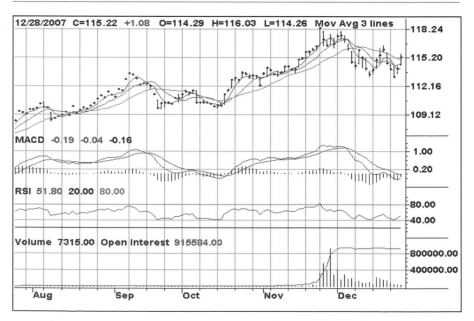

Source: Charts provided courtesy of TradingCharts.com: http//futures.tradingcharts.com; created with SuperCharts by Omega Research © 1997.

So if you convert U.S. dollars into British pounds, you receive about 0.51 pounds per dollar. And if you convert British pounds back to U.S. dollars, each pound would get you about $1.95. These rates change daily, which is where the currency futures contract comes into play. In today's global economy, international commerce has made currency exchange very important. For example, overseas currency exchange affects even those companies listed on the U.S. stock exchanges, especially if those companies are multinational. Companies like Coca-Cola and MacDonald's, for example, sell in many countries and generate most of their revenue overseas. As a direct consequence of this, as the dollar's value relative to other currencies falls, these multinationals are likely to see increased profits from their direct sales in those countries.

Valuable Resource: To check exchange rates and conversion between any two currencies, go to www.x-rates.com.

There are many currencies on which futures are traded. Among these are the British pound (symbol £), which is denominated in decimal units of 100 pence. This decimalization became effective on February 15, 1971, replacing the previous pound-based system of shillings (with 20 shillings to the pound) and pence (12 pence to the shilling, thus 240 pence to the pound). The pound represents about one-third of global currency reserves, following the U.S. dollar and the euro. It is also the fourth most traded foreign exchange currency, after the U.S. dollar, euro and Japanese yen. Figure 14-2 summarizes the March 2008 futures contract for the British pound as of December 2007.

The euro (symbol €) is the official European Union (EU) currency, and is used in 15 countries (Austria, Belgium, Cyprus, Finland, France, Germany, Greece, Ireland, Italy, Luxembourg, Malta, The Netherlands, Portugal, Slovenia, and Spain). Among European countries not using the euro are the UK, Denmark, and Sweden. Many other currencies are pegged to the euro, making it the currency for 500 million people around the world. As of the end of 2006, there were 610 billion in circulation (about equal to US $802 billion), giving it the highest circulation value of any currency.

The euro trades in decimal values, with 100 cents to the euro. Coins include the €2, €1, €.50, €.20, €0.10, €0.05, €0.02, and

FIGURE 14.2. BRITISH POUND—MARCH

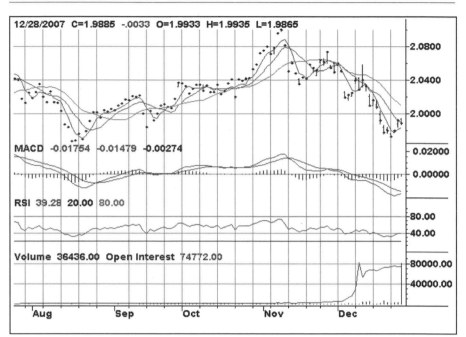

Source: Charts provided courtesy of TradingCharts.com: http//futures.tradingcharts.com; created with SuperCharts by Omega Research © 1997.

€0.01. Euro banknotes are issued in €500, €200, €100, €50, €20, €10, and €5 denominations. Low and high exchange rates from 1999 to 2008 of euros in U.S. dollars, according to the European Central Bank (www.ecb.int), were:

| Year | Lowest | | | Highest | |
	Date	Rate		Date	Rate
1999	12-03	$1.0015		01-05	$1.1790
2000	10-26	0.8252		01-06	1.0388
2001	07-06	0.8384		01-05	0.9545
2002	01-28	0.8578		12-31	1.0487
2003	01-08	1.0377		12-31	1.2630
2004	05-14	1.1802		12-28	1.3633
2005	11-15	1.1667		01-03	1.3507
2006	01-02	1.1826		12-05	1.3331
2007	01-12	1.2893		11-27	1.4874
2008	01-21	1.4482		01-14	1.4895

This chart demonstrates a one-decade slide in the U.S. dollar versus the euro. While the original exchange rate was one to one, the euro has risen ever since. Figure 14-3 shows the March 2008 futures contract for the euro as of December 2007.

The Japanese yen (symbol ¥) is the official currency of Japan, and is the third most traded after the U.S. dollar and the euro. It is also a popular reserve currency in many nations. Figure 14-4 shows the March 2008 futures contract for the Japanese yen as of December 2007.

The U.S. Dollar Index (USDX) is a popular index of the nation's currency as traded against a basket of foreign currencies (British pound, euro, Japanese yen, Canadian dollar, Swedish krona, and the Swiss franc). This index was begun in March 1973 soon after the Bretton Woods system was done away with. This was a form of international monetary management entered into by the world's industrialized nations after World War II. The original pur-

FIGURE 14.3. EURO—MARCH

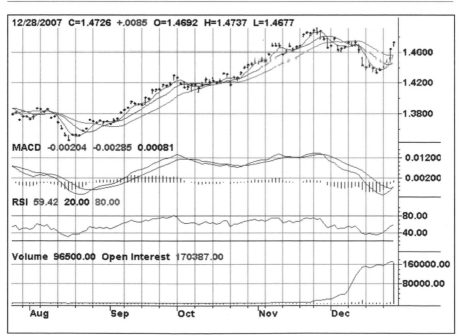

Source: Charts provided courtesy of TradingCharts.com: http//futures.tradingcharts.com; created with SuperCharts by Omega Research © 1997.

FIGURE 14.4. JAPANESE YEN—MARCH

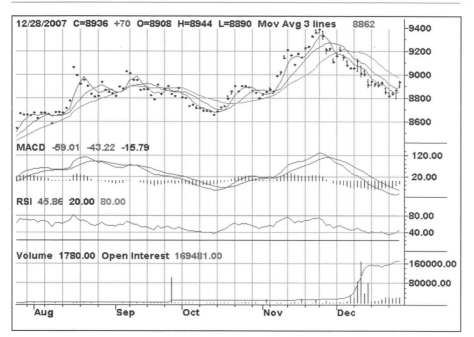

Source: Charts provided courtesy of TradingCharts.com: http//futures.tradingcharts.com; created with SuperCharts by Omega Research © 1997.

pose was to help nations rebuild from the war, and the agreement also formed the International Bank for Reconstruction and Development (IBRD, now reformed as the World Bank), and the International Monetary Fund (IMF). The Bretton Woods system attempted to regulate exchange rates pegged to gold valuation; however, when the United States went off the gold standard in 1971, the system collapsed. The U.S. Dollar Index formed shortly after Bretton Woods failed, with the original value set at an index of 100.00. By the end of 2007, the index was at about 76. Figure 14-5 shows the March contract as of December 2007.

Index Futures

In February 1982, the first-ever stock index was created on the Kansas City Board of Trade. That was the Value Line Composite Index, including the 1,700 stocks that Value Line tracked and ana-

FIGURE 14.5. U.S. DOLLAR INDEX—MARCH

Source: Charts provided courtesy of TradingCharts.com: http//futures.tradingcharts.com; created with SuperCharts by Omega Research © 1997.

lyzed. Shortly after this new idea, many other stock-based indices were introduced. Today, you can trade index futures on stocks as well as on futures.

The index itself tracks a specifically identified grouping of stocks. So the New York Stock Exchange Composite Index or the S&P 500 Index are among the popular indices tracked in this manner. In addition to buying shares in these index groupings, you can also trade futures on them. Futures on broad indices are not valuable as hedge instruments if your portfolio is small or limited in scope; however, for a diverse portfolio that involves broad market participation, index futures can be valuable. For example, if your portfolio includes long positions in a broad mutual fund account, shorting a stock index future is one way to hedge such a portfolio.

In addition to using futures on stock-based indices, you can also buy or sell futures on indices tracking the futures market. In other words, you can trade futures on the broad futures market itself, which overcomes the problem of diversification. If you originally plan to buy or sell futures contracts, you face the problem of a very extensive market with several subclassifications. In addition, direct trading is awkward and expensive; so as a result, many traders have been attracted to futures indices like the well-known Reuters/Jeffries CRB Index (CRB) or the Goldman Sachs Commodity Index (GSCI). Both of these include a diversified portfolio of futures contracts.

Going a step beyond buying or selling shares of the index is the concept of trading in futures on those commodity-based indices. The CRB, for example, is comprised of more energy futures than any other subclass. It also holds futures in agricultural, precious metals, livestock, and tropicals/imports. In the 2005–2007 period when futures values were rising strongly across a broad front, the CRB performed quite well; and buying futures in that index is one way to leverage capital and benefit from market trends.

So when you believe futures prices are going to rise, you may benefit from buying futures in the CRB. This achieves market-wide participation for far less money than would be required to buy actual shares. If you believe the market is going to decline, you can sell the same futures. Hedging and other forms of speculative trading are also possible. The use of futures on an index of commodities is probably the most practical way to diversify and to leverage capital.

Figure 14-6 shows the March 2008 contract for the CRB futures contract as of December 2007.

Futures on stock indices include the DJIA, which is comprised of 30 industrial stocks. The futures contract tracks this index, which is the most popular index in the entire stock market. The DJIA futures contract dollar value is equal to 10 times the index value. So when the DJIA is at 13,000, the DJIA futures contract is assigned a value of $130,000. So a 100-point move creates a change in the futures contract of $1,000.

This kind of leverage is very exciting to traders who follow "The Dow," as the DJIA is often called. You gain an interest in all 30 of the DJIA stocks by trading in the futures contract. A comparison to direct purchase of stocks makes the point. In a typical stock-

FIGURE 14.6. CRB FUTURES—MARCH

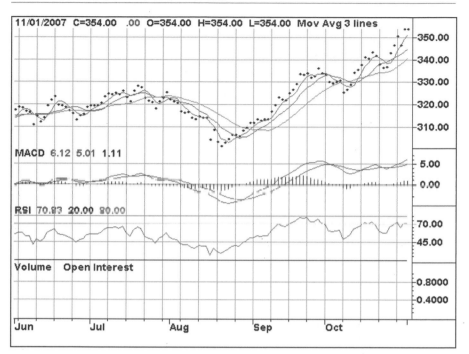

Source: Charts provided courtesy of TradingCharts.com: http//futures.tradingcharts.com; created with SuperCharts by Omega Research © 1997.

based margin account, you can leverage up to 50%, so with a $50,000 deposit you could own up to $100,000 worth of stock. But if you buy DJIA futures, you can cover the same level of stock participation for much less money. The level required varies as the DJIA changes its level. Another advantage to trading DJIA futures is that you can short the index far more easily than would be possible to short all 30 companies in the index.

Futures on stock indices are valuable for pure speculation or to hedge portfolio positions involving a range of the market (such as equity mutual fund holdings). Given the volatility of the market in recent years, the appeal of a futures contract on the DJIA is high. With the market often moving well in excess of 100 points ($1,000 change in the futures contract), a form of swing trading with the DJIA makes a lot of sense. Swing traders like to move in and out of positions in a three- to five-day period, and they base the timing of their decisions on the scope of movement (in stocks or indices).

Because of the multiplier of 10, the volatility of the DJIA makes the futures contract a viable instrument for swing trading. It also makes it easy and convenient to play with long and short sides of market movements.

Figure 14-7 shows the March 2008 DJIA futures contract as of December 2007.

Many people who limit their investment range to a stock portfolio may benefit by following the DJIA futures contract. By watching overall volume, MACD, and RSI as well as the direct tracking of the futures contract, you can judge the market on a technical basis, and time stock-based decisions using the futures contract trends.

Another popular index is the New York Stock Exchange Composite Index. This is an index of all common stocks of companies listed on the NYSE. On June 1, 2007, the index went above 10,000 points for the first time, twice the 500-point level it was assigned

FIGURE 14.7. DJIA FUTURES—MARCH

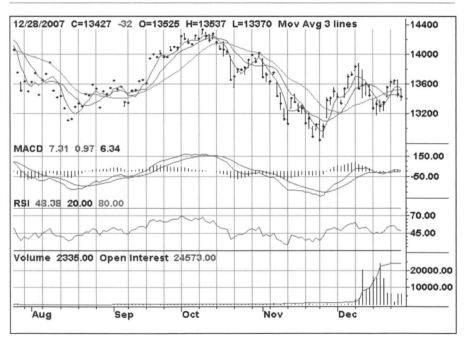

Source: Charts provided courtesy of TradingCharts.com: http//futures.tradingcharts.com; created with SuperCharts by Omega Research © 1997.

only four years earlier. The index itself trades as an ETF under the name iShares NYSE Composite Index Fund (NYC). The futures contract enables you to trade long or short on the NYSE Composite, based on the ETF trend and level. Figure 14-8 summarizes the March 2008 contract as of December 2007.

Another popular stock-based index is the S&P 500, which includes 500 large-cap corporations. These companies' stock trades on both the NYSE and NASDAQ exchanges and, following the DJIA, the S&P 500 is the second-most popular market index. While the DJIA 30 industrial stocks are viewed as reliable indicators of market trends, the S&P 500—which is far broader—is viewed by many as an indicator of the strength or weakness in the U.S. economy. The index is included as part of the Index of Leading Indicators tracked by the Conference Board (*www.conferenceboard.org*), which is used to predict economic trends. So the S&P 500 is important not only for market trends, but also for broader

FIGURE 14.8. NYSE COMPOSITE INDEX—MARCH

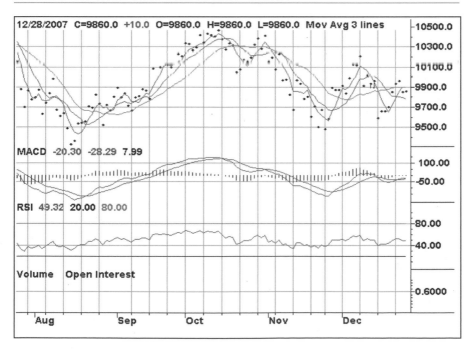

Source: Charts provided courtesy of TradingCharts.com: http//futures.tradingcharts.com; created with SuperCharts by Omega Research © 1997.

economic trends as well. The S&P 500 is also used as a comparative indicator to judge mutual fund performance.

Rather than having to buy shares of all 500 companies in this index, investors can buy shares of an ETF that includes the entire index. The iShares S&P 500 (IVV) is one of several ETFs tracking this index. In addition, many mutual fund companies offer index funds tracking the S&P. The first among this group was Vanguard Group's S&P tracking fund (VFINX). Futures on the S&P are traded on the CME. Figure 14-9 shows the March 2008 contract as of December 2007.

■ Individual Stock Futures

Trading in individual stock futures contracts normally refer to an underlying value equal to 100 shares of stock. When you trade futures instead of stock, you do not earn dividends on those shares, and you do not have voting rights. However, the futures contract

FIGURE 14.9. S&P 500 INDEX—MARCH

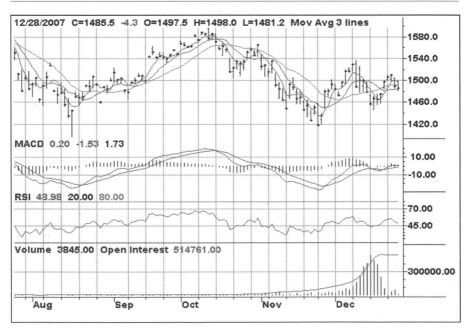

Source: Charts provided courtesy of TradingCharts.com: http//futures.tradingcharts.com; created with SuperCharts by Omega Research © 1997.

can be purchased with smaller margin levels and for much less money. For stocks bought on margin, a 50% cash requirement applies; futures on stocks require only 20% cash. This leverage increases your margin range. In addition, because futures cost less than stocks, you can control about 2 1/2 times more stock than you can through direct purchase.

In addition, you can short a futures contract without needing to borrow shares of stock, as you do when you short stock through your brokerage account. Speculators interested in short sales or hedgers desiring protection of long positions benefit from selling futures on stock because, like other futures, the contract values diminish as the delivery date approaches. So the original sales price declines, meaning the position can be closed profitably.

Futures act in many of the same ways as options; but there are important differences. First of all, a futures contract requires fulfillment of the contract, whereas option buyers have only the right and not the obligation to buy. However, actual delivery is avoided by closing out a contract or by rolling it forward, just like any futures contract. Some traders prefer futures over options due to potential profits and advantageous margin rules. While options can also be rolled forward to avoid exercise, the differential in breakeven point can be slim. Many option rolls are done simply to avoid exercise, but involve little or no profit and, at times, a small loss.

In the past, single stock futures were not allowed in the United States, mainly because the Commodity Futures Trading Commission (CFTC) and the Securities and Exchange Commission (SEC) could not decide which agency would have regulatory oversight in this market. It was not until 2002 that the two agencies sharing jurisdiction resolved the problem.

This chapter concludes the discussion of financial types of futures and options on those futures. As you can see, the variety of methods available for playing the futures market enables you to pick an appropriate risk level based on your knowledge, experience, and willingness to place capital at risk. These potential alternatives broaden the methods for being involved in futures, diversifying and allocating your portfolio, and managing risk.

CONCLUSION

A ny form of investing or trading demands skill and knowledge. The futures market is among the most complex of all markets, and this prevents many people from taking advantage of it in risk appropriate ways.

When you consider the many avenues for futures investing, it becomes clear that you may be able to match a strategic approach to your own requirements. For example, as this book has shown, you can trade futures contracts directly; trade shares of index funds and exchange-traded funds (ETFs); and even buy options on futures contracts. You can also invest in commodity sectors by buying shares of sector-based ETFs, rather than buying stocks in a sector's leading corporation. Therefore, you are not limited to just trading futures contracts. In fact, many experienced investors and traders are less than comfortable in this market, due to the high cost of trading and, compared to stock trading, the complex methods of entering and executing trades. The alternatives solve this problem.

In addition to being able to match a method of going into the futures market, you can also accomplish many goals in your investment program that may include the futures market. For example, concerns about the value of the U.S. dollar may lead you to currency futures or to focusing on sectors with international markets. If you are aware of high energy costs and future energy demands, the energy futures (the most actively traded) are quite popular, and futures indices as well as ETFs and sector funds also address this interest.

Futures are useful instruments in their many avenues for a wide range of investment and trading risk levels. The risk taker can certainly speculate in either long or short positions through commodity brokers. More conservative investors can hedge their stock or mutual fund portfolios with short positions in futures or in ETFs and indices spread throughout the subsectors of the futures market. And using a variety of these methods, futures serve as an effective way to hedge against economic changes, including the threats of both inflation and recession. Even the most conservative investor can use the futures market in its many forms to diversify beyond stocks, bonds, the money market, and real estate; and to broaden an asset allocation program.

As the global economy expands and a growing number of U.S.-based corporations become multinational, the complexities of commodity costs as well as currency exchange and interest rate levels make futures more essential than ever before, not only to institutional investors and large corporations, but also to individuals. For example, you cannot possibly know what markets are going to look like in a few years, so buying stock is a high-risk venture on its own. For example, you may buy shares in an energy company in the hope that its future stock price will be higher. But if you are wrong, then your stock will lose value. By selling calls or buying puts on an energy sector ETF or a commodity index fund focusing heavily in energy futures, you can hedge your long stock position. The limited risks of this market approach make the strategy prudent. At the same time, it eliminates the higher risk and cost of trading energy futures directly.

You can apply the same approach to any market sector, and the interaction between stock market sectors and the futures market is inescapable. In addition, the subsectors of the futures market are also interdependent. The example used in this book was that of corn futures. Food prices rose when the demand for ethanol fuel placed additional demands on the corn crop. In this example, corn-based ethanol might affect energy prices in one direction, while other industries would suffer higher prices. Corn is a basic food source and a major cattle feed base, as well as being used in numerous industrial applications. The point to remember is that *everything* is interdependent, and in the modern global community, this reality will only expand as progress continues.

In the not-so-distant past, it was possible to create an illusion of isolation from the rest of the world. Domestic production and consumption, a focused futures market, and lack of interest in the supply and demand of the international community has never been absolute, and international trade has always existed. However, the modern recognition that these dependencies are ever-present is a major change from the past. Today, no one can really ignore the fact that all markets, especially the futures market, rely upon and are affected by events and economic change around the world.

INDEX